INSIGHTS INTO ISLAM

Contemporary and Historical Studies on Islam and Christianity

Edited by

MICHAEL RAITER

Occasional Papers in the Study of Islam
and Other Faiths No. 3 (2012)

The Centre for the Study of Islam
and Other Faiths (CSIOF)

Occasional Papers in the Study of Islam and Other Faiths
No 3. (2012)

ISSN 1836-9782

Copyright © 2012 by Melbourne School of Theology Press.
All rights reserved. 2016 Reprint.

Editor
Michael Raiter

Assistant Editor
Kathryn Simon

Editorial Board
Andy Bannister, Brian Edgar, Kevin Giles, Tony Lane, Sean Oliver-Dee, Darrell Paproth, David Price, Michael Raiter, Steve Walton, Ted Woods.

Production and Cover Design
Ho-yuin Chan

Publishing Services
Published by Melbourne School of Theology Press.
Thank you to Mark Durie for his publishing services.

Centre for the Study of Islam and Other Faiths
Melbourne School of Theology
5 Burwood Highway, Wantirna, Victoria 3152, Australia.
PO Box 6257, Vermont Sth, Victoria 3133, Australia
Ph: +61 3 9881 7800, Fax: +61 3 9800 0121
csiof@mst.edu.au, www.mst.edu.au

People involved in the field of Muslim-Christian relations are welcome to submit related items to the Editor for consideration for publishing in the CSIOF Occasional Papers.

Opinions and conclusions published in the CSIOF Occasional Papers are those of the authors and do not necessarily represent the views of the Editor or the CSIOF. The Occasional Papers is purely an information medium, to inform interested parties of religious trends, discussions and debates. The Occasional Papers do not intend in any way to actively promote hatred of any religion or its followers.

CONTENTS

INTRODUCTION – INSIGHTS INTO ISLAM THE BIBLE AND THE QUR'AN: POST 9/11 PERSPECTIVES	1
Michael Raiter	5
THE HISTORY OF MODERN ISLAMOPHOBIA	
Anthony McRoy	27
AN EXEGETICAL STUDY OF THE QUR'ANIC TEACHINGS ON THE JEWISH PEOPLE	
Jannah Walters	37
AUSTRALIAN ISLAM AND THE BATTERED WIFE SYNDROME	
Bernie Power	53
USING THE BIBLE IN DA'WA	
Denis Savelyev	67
THE REAL STORY BEHIND THE MASSACRE OF THE BANU QURAYZA	
Daniel Janosik	97
ISLAM IN EUROPE: CONCERNS, TRENDS AND DEBATES	
Peter Riddell	115
A CONTRAST BETWEEN EVANGELICAL AND ISLAMIC PERSPECTIVES TOWARDS PEOPLE WITH DISABILITIES WITH IMPLICATIONS FOR EVANGELICAL AND MUSLIM OUTREACH TO THE DISABLED	
Ruth Turner	135
INTEGRAL MISSION IN A DISINTEGRATING WORLD	
David Williams	165
NOTES FOR CONTRIBUTORS	181

Introduction

Insights into Islam

Contemporary and Historical Studies on Islam & Christianity

Since the establishment of the Centre for the Study of Islam and Other Faiths (CSIOF) at Melbourne School of Theology (then the Bible College of Victoria) in 2008, serious academic research into the leading world religions, most notably Islam, has been one of the Centre's main concerns. Annually, the CSIOF publishes both the *CSIOF Bulletin*, a collection of shorter articles and reviews, and the *Occasional Papers*, which contain more substantial studies on comparative religion. The *Occasional Papers* provide a vehicle both for faculty of the CSIOF and post-graduate students to publish the fruit of their studies.

This latest publication, *Insights into Islam: Contemporary and Historical Studies on Islam and Christianity* comprises nine papers which, while diverse in their subject matter, are driven by the same concern: an honest investigation into historical and contemporary Islam which is free from the shackles of facile political correctness on the one hand, and uninformed rhetoric on the other. All the contributors are convinced that the emergence of a vigorous and politically active Islam is one of the great challenges facing the world today; all the more so given that many within Islam are deeply resistant to any substantial critique of both its sacred text and Prophet, and its contemporary expression. It is imperative that, like every other religion and worldview, Islam submit itself to honest and rigorous academic analysis. It is critical that the *Qur'an* be subject to the same historical, critical and exegetical analysis that other ancient texts face. This is all the more important, given the mixed messages that are consistently presented from Islamic spokespeople regarding Islam's attitude to those who do not share its faith and commitments.

The publications of the CSIOF have two main foci. First, the Centre provides a conducive environment for the study of the sacred texts, and historical development, of the leading world religions. Second, it is concerned to investigate and analyze contemporary social and political trends in these religions. When it comes to Islam, again, one finds a lack of sober analysis from both sides of the divide. Both radical Muslims and non-Muslim prophets of doom forecast the imminent moral and political collapse of the post-Christian West and its replacement by Islamic governments enacting *shariah* law. Clear thinking based on extensive and reliable research is vitally needed.

In the light of this, *Insights into Islam* presents nine papers on historical and contemporary Islam. Mind you, even those papers with an historical focus have an implicit contemporary agenda. In a sense, the first paper, which is a comparative review of three books on the Bible and the Qur'an, really serves as an introduction to the whole book, as it raises the broader questions of the true character of Islam, its relationship with Christianity, and how mutual understanding and co-operation can be furthered. In the first of the investigations into contemporary Islam, Anthony McRoy traces the rise of the phenomenon of 'Islamophobia' since the late 1980's. Given the repeated accusation that Western non-Muslims are unreasonably Islamophobic, this essay provides a necessary wider historical perspective. One of the most contentious of all debates about the historical Muhammad is his attitude towards, and treatment of, the Jews. In the first of two studies on this issue Jannah Walters provides an exegetical analysis of two Sura, one from the Medinan period and one from the Meccan, both of which are representative of Muhammad's attitude towards the Jews. Addressing the contemporary Australian context lecturer in Islam at the CSIOF, Bernie Power, challenges Muslims to address the predilection to violence within Islam both in the domestic and the geopolitical realm. Anti-Christian polemic has long been an important tool in Islam's 'evangelistic' engagement with Christianity. In 'Using the Bible in Da'wa' Denis Savelyev provides a comprehensive survey of four important and influential books written by Muslims in the past 80 years and used to attack the Christian's confidence in the Bible. In the second article which examines Muhammad's attitude towards Jews, Daniel Janosik critically examines the emotionally charged issue of 'The Real Story Behind the Massacre of the Banu Qurayza'; Muhammad's infamous massacre of over 600 Jews. In response to concern about the growth of Islam in Europe, in an important study Dean of the CSIOF, Peter Riddell, examines 'Islam in Europe: Concerns, Trends and Debates'. One of the most important social issues of this generation has been the plight of the disabled. There has been a growing recognition by society more widely of the considerable disadvantages faced by this significant minority group in our society. In the light of this, Ruth Turner contrasts the attitudes and practices of evangelical Christians and Muslims towards the disabled, and then examines how representatives from both faiths express in practice their theology of the disabled. In the final paper David Williams takes us back to a broader context for the entire discussion by examining the contentious issue of 'Integral Mission in a Disintegrating World'. This reassessment of the nature of the Christian mission in the light of the contemporary debate provides a fitting conclusion to this stimulating collection of essays.

The publication of this collection coincides with the growing uncertainty regarding the outcome of what has become known as the 'Arab Spring'; the popular overthrow of Middle Eastern despotic regimes. It seems realistic more than pessimistic to suggest that the future for the Middle East will not be the emergence of anything resembling Western-style democracies, where the rights of minorities are recognized and protected, and where there is genuine freedom of thought and speech. Rather, we face the likely spectre of a series of conservative Islamic governments which, to varying degrees, will find in their Islamic traditions the ideological authority for their national governance. Should this eventuate it will have repercussions for the whole world. In the light of this, discussions about the complementarity of Islam and Christianity, the perception of Islam in the West, Islam's compatibility with Western values, and Muhammad and Islam's treatment of minorities, take on a particular relevance and significance.

Michael Raiter
Editor

The Bible and the Qur'an: Post 9/11 Perspectives

Michael Raiter

Melbourne School of Theology

Introduction: Writing in the Shadow of 9/11

I am writing this article on 9/11, the ninth month of 2011. In other words, 10 years after 'the day that changed the world'. While some might question the accuracy of that statement (for many in the world, life goes on unchanged) there can be no doubt that these brazen and appalling acts of mass murder profoundly shaped the next ten years globally. While the wars in Iraq and Afghanistan are winding down, at the same time the 'war on terror' continues unabated. Acts of violence conducted in the name of Islam continue without any sign of diminishing, and the surprising and cataclysmic events that continue to unfold in the Middle East with the domino-like overthrow of entrenched Muslim governments, raise the spectre of a very uncertain future for that part of the world. It is by no means certain that the longed-for emergence of Western style democratic regimes will replace the autocratic rules of men like Mubarak and Gaddafi. Equally plausible is the ascendancy of deeply conservative Islamic governments ruled by mullahs and Shariah law.

The interest of this brief article is to examine two books written in the wake of 9/11. Both books deal with the same theme: a comparison of the two texts held sacred by their adherents, the Bible and the Qur'an. Of course, the comparison is all the more interesting and important because of the thematic and topical overlap of both revered texts. Both holy books purport to be the revelations from the one, true God who, initially, revealed himself to Abraham, Isaac and Jacob. Both sacred texts report on many of the same events in Israel's history although, of course, the recounting, and the significance derived from these events, usually differs very widely. Of the two books to be examined one is self-confessedly from the more liberal wing of the Christian church, and that is *Noah's Other Son: Bridging the Gap Between the Bible and the Qur'an* by Brian Arthur Brown. By way of comparison we will examine Michael Lodahl's, *Claiming Abraham: Reading the Bible and the Qur'an Side by Side,* which places itself firmly in the evangelical tradition. Of interest to us is not just the conclusions the authors draw from their comparative analyses, but also the degree to which we can detect the impact of 9/11 on their studies.

By way of contrast, though, I want to begin this analysis by examining a far older treatment of the same topic. Recently the series, 'Exploring the House of Islam in the Period of Western Ascendancy 1800-1945' has republished a relatively little-known book, *Christianity and Islam: The Bible and the Koran* by British scholar and clergyman, W.R.W. Stephens.[1] An Oxford graduate, the Rev Dr William Richard Wood Stephens (1839-1902) was the quintessential clergyman/scholar. A keen historian and biographer, Stephens published several books and numerous pamphlets. His ecclesiastical career climaxed with his appointment as Dean of Winchester Cathedral in 1894. This particular book is based on the four Advent lectures he delivered almost a decade earlier, in 1876, at Chichester Cathedral. What makes Stephen's study particularly interesting is that he writes - like the contemporary two scholars we will examine - as a layman in Islamic studies; he did not know Arabic and had not served in the Muslim world. Further, he was liberal in his political inclinations and, therefore, could be expected to present a more measured treatment of Islam. Finally, like many writers on Islam today, he was led to address the topic of Islam and Christianity because the topic was 'salutary and opportune', particularly in light of the 'Eastern question', which may be a reference to the political and moral decline of the Ottoman Empire or, what was known then, as 'the Turkish problem'.[2] In short, Stephens' work provides an ideal foil to our examination of the works of Brown and Lodahl, as it is free of the bonds of contemporary political correctness (while, of course, being equally subject to the constraints of its own day).

1. The Bible and the Qur'an: A 19th Century Perspective

If *The Bible and the Koran* finds any echo in modern analyses of Islam, it is in the provocative and polemical writings of renowned

---

[1] W.R.W. Stephens, *Christianity and Islam: The Bible and the Koran* (Piscataway, NJ: Georgias Press).

[2] From the introduction by Clinton Bennett, *The Bible and the Koran*, xxiii-xxiv.

critics like Ibn Warraq and Robert Spencer. Indeed, in parts Stephens' rhetoric seems, to modern ears, more akin to the abusive ridicule of militant atheists like Richard Dawkins and Christopher Hitchens.

Space does not permit an analysis of all four lectures contained in the book. The first is a comparison of the respective origins of Christianity and Islam, and an overview of Muhammad's life and character. On the one hand, Stephens concludes that any objective observer cannot but stand in awe and admiration at a man who "had achieved so great and wonderful a work",[3] particularly in ridding Mecca of its idols. Yet at the same time, Stephens finds repellent his "repulsive cruelties",[4] "the picture of mingled fanaticism and sensuality which Mahomet presents to us in later years",[5] and a moral sense that, by the end of his life was "confused and perverted".[6] For Stephens, diametrically opposed to this is the Founder of the Christian Religion.

Stephens' third lecture compares the moral teaching of the Bible and the Qur'an. In summary,

> The moral motive of Islam is a solemn sense of duty of obedience and submission to an Almighty Ruler; whereas the moral motive of Christianity is love to an Almighty Father, an all-sympathising Redeemer, Brother and Friend. [7]

The final lecture examines 'The Practical Results of Islam and Christianity' concluding, perhaps not surprisingly, that while Islam was an improvement on barbarism, "among nations already acquainted with the civilization of the Roman Empire and the light of the Christian religion...we are compelled by the facts of history to decline believing that in these cases Islam, viewed as a whole,

---

[3] Stephens, *The Bible and the Koran*, 37.

[4] Stephens, *The Bible and the Koran*, 37.

[5] Stephens, *The Bible and the Koran*, 42.

[6] Stephens, *The Bible and the Koran*, 43.

[7] Stephens, *The Bible and the Koran*, 124.

has been anything but a complete evil."[8] The remainder of the chapter is a defence of this assertion.

But it is Stephens' comparison of the theology of the Bible and the Qur'an, the subject of his second lecture, which is of most interest and relevance to us. Essentially, the chapter is a comparison of the style and structure, and the content of the two holy books. With the Bible Stephens finds that the unity of its aim and expression is not compromised by the fact of its diversity; many books, different forms (genres) yet "essentially one: inasmuch as the thread of one divine purpose and design runs through the whole".[9] By contrast, the Qur'an he finds to be fragmentary, incoherent and monotonous. Further, for Stephens the fact that the Bible is so amenable to translation bespeaks its divine origin. Yet again, the Qur'an fails this test: "Nothing, however, more forcibly illustrates the poverty of the Koran...than its inability to stand the test of translation".[10] While acknowledging the purported majesty of the Qur'an in its original Arabic, stripped of this by translation one is left with a book that is "insufferably dull and commonplace".[11]

With respect to the teaching of the Qur'an, Stephens recognises it extols the wonders of the natural world, and he appreciates the beauty and truth of those passages which affirm the omnipresence, omniscience and justice of God. Yet, for Stephens, when all the virtues of the Qur'an are enumerated we are still left with a book that presents a pure, rigid and austere monotheism. He compares the teaching of both books on predestination, holy war, and the Holy Spirit, in each instance finding the Qur'an's revelations cold and comfortless. In its historical reportage of events like the exodus and the settlement of Canaan he finds the book of Muhammad, "(so) overlaid with such a mass of tedious legendary rubbish, that the mind of the reader becomes fatigued and bewildered, and

---

[8] Stephens, *The Bible and the Koran*, 132-3.

[9] Stephens, *The Bible and the Koran*, 53.

[10] Stephens, *The Bible and the Koran*, 60.

[11] Stephens, *The Bible and the Koran*, 60.

thankfully escapes from the fantastic shadows of Fairyland into the serene daylight of real history".[12]

In summary, Stephens finds the Qur'an a clumsy production and,

> ...to suppose that Gabriel was sent from heaven to reveal the childish absurdities which it contains, would be an insult to the character and work of angels. [13]

Reflections on the Bible and the Koran

What do we say about *The Bible and the Koran*? First, it betrays the fact that its author is writing as a distant, objective observer of Islam, and not an evangelist living and working amongst Muslims. One would be hard pressed to find the kind of inflammatory polemic that marks many pages of *The Bible and the Koran* in the writings of Muslim missionaries Samuel Zwemer or W.H. Temple Gairdner.

Secondly, the book also gives us an insight into Stephens' political and theological context. Presumably, as a politically liberal High Churchman he was addressing an audience that would have been considered informed and open-minded and, yet, there appeared to have been a high tolerance for the kind of polemic that marks this work. The unrestrained nature of his attacks upon the Qur'an and its founder, which today seem crude and offensive, apparently found an appreciative audience in the latter half of the nineteenth-century. Of course, Stephens saw his treatment of Islam as just and fair-minded and would have taken umbrage at the suggestion that he was in any way vilifying his subject. Further, it also suggests that as early as 1870 English-speaking people were sufficiently concerned about distant Islam as to make it a matter of public debate.

Thirdly, even the most sympathetic Christian reader would be hard-pressed not to find a degree of bias in his comparative study. For example, while some parts of the Bible reach great heights in poetry and prose, all scholars agree that its claim to divine inspiration is not compromised by the occasional prosaic nature of its writing. The New Testament writers wrote, not in classical Greek, but *koine*

---

[12] Stephens, *The Bible and the Koran*, 74.

[13] Stephens, *The Bible and the Koran*, 85.

Greek; the Greek of the marketplace. And even the apostle Peter found his brother Paul's arguments, at times, complex and contorted. Yet Stephens can only find good things to say about his own faith while, as Clinton Bennett, the editor, acknowledges, any praise of Islam is grudgingly given.

Finally, it is striking to read Clinton Bennett's introduction to the book, which almost serves as a justification for re-publishing a work that, "may give new life to old ideas that do little to improve understanding between Muslims and non-Muslims".[14] The book's value appears to lie in the insights it gives to us today into the Christian/Western mindset of the 19th century, a mindset which largely unquestioned the uniqueness of Christianity. Bennett is clearly unhappy with Stephens' unwillingness to allow for the fact that Muhammad had an intimate relationship with God and that Islam has genuine spiritual depth. Of course, it may be that our discomfort with much of Stephen's rhetoric is as much a reflection of our own pluralistic and inclusive religious worldview, which is so pervasive in Western society and so intolerant of any exclusive truth claims. In the end, Stephens' concluding remarks on Christianity and Islam seem measured, generous and orthodox:

> There is a line between us; if we can persuade them to cross the line and to be one with us, we will receive them with open arms; if they will not cross it, let us shake hands over the line, and work hand in hand whenever they will move in a parallel direction with us. But do not let us pretend that there is no line, that Christianity is only a few shades better than Mohammadanism, the Bible only 'as a whole' better than the Koran, and that the difference between the two religions is one not of kind but only of degree.[15]

2. The Bible and the Qur'an: Post 9/11 Analyses

Noah's Other Son: Bridging the Gap Between the Bible and the Qur'an

"Where were you on September 11th?" With this question, Brian Arthur Brown, a minister in the United Church of Canada, both begins his comparative study of the Bible and the Qur'an, and sets

---

[14] Stephens, *The Bible and the Koran*, xxvi.

[15] Stephens, *The Bible and the Koran*, 167.

the contextual framework for the study. Brown claims that from 9/11 onwards his own preaching changed. A new agenda shaped the form of his ministry. His overriding concern was to work towards the reconciliation of the three great monotheistic faiths. He writes,

> The hot issue in the world of the new century is the ongoing family feud involving Muslims, Christians and Jews...Abraham's dysfunctional family.[16]

The particular contribution this book seeks to make in order to bring about peace between these warring religious cousins is a comparative examination of their two key holy books. One of the first things that strikes a reader of *Noah's Other Son,* is how very different Brown's presuppositional starting point is from a book like Stephens', *The Bible and the Koran.* Like Stephens, Brown does not speak from the experience of working in a Muslim environment yet, unlike Stephens, he lives and serves in a multi- religious context and, from time to time, invites leaders of other religious traditions to teach and preach in his church. In short, he approaches Islam from a much more sympathetic standpoint. "In truth", he writes, "Islam is beautiful; the problem is in the eyes of the beholders."[17] Secondly, he is ready to grant the Qur'an the status of being an inspired, authoritative Scripture. For Brown, there is little question that Muhammad was an authentic spokesman for God. He observes that, "even a cursory reading of the Qur'an makes it clear that it is like the third book in the series, ostensibly from the same source".[18] The fact that many other readers of the Bible and the Qur'an, both Christian and Muslim, after in-depth study, draw a very different conclusion, suggests that this statement tells us more about Brown's presuppositions than any real or perceived thematic unity between the books.

Following the Biblical chronology, *Noah's Other Son* compares the accounts of both the major and minor Biblical characters, concluding with an analysis of Muhammad. We cannot examine in

---

[16] Brian Arthur Brown, *Noah's Other Son: Bridging the Gap Between the Bible and the Qur'an* (New York: Continuum, 2007), 13.

[17] Brown, *Noah's Other Son,* 9.

[18] Brown, *Noah's Other Son,* 31.

any detail Brown's comparative studies, but we will just reflect upon one, the story that forms the title for the book, Noah, the flood and his sons. In terms of narrative history, the major point of disagreement between the Bible and the Qur'an revolves around the fate of Noah's son, Canaan. In short, according to the Bible Noah and *all* his family were saved from the flood in the ark, while the Quranic version affirms that his son, who one of the Hadiths identifies as Canaan, chooses to stay with his friends, the unbelievers and, as a consequence is swept away in the flood. According to Genesis 9:18 Canaan was the son of Noah's second son, Ham. Potentially, this kind of discrepancy creates a problem for writers like Brown who wish to affirm the essential theological unity of the Jewish, Christian and Muslim Scriptures, and the divine inspiration behind them all. Of course, it is not a problem for most Muslims and Christians. For Muslims, the Bible, both Old Testament and New Testament, is a corrupted text. It has been deliberately changed by mischievous Jews and Christians. For Christians, Muhammad was simply mistaken. He'd heard from Jewish sources various Old Testament accounts and in this case, as in many others, he was confused. This illustrates, for many Christians, the essential unreliability of the Qur'an.

But for those who wish to affirm the sacredness, inspiration, and essential harmony of the Bible and the Qur'an how, then, does one reconcile such a glaring difference in historical reportage? For Brown, rather than the two accounts being adversarial they are, in fact, complementary. Brown argues that Ham named his son 'Canaan' in memory of his brother who was lost. Further, Brown maintains that seeing the complementarity of the two accounts helps to resolve a long-standing hermeneutical problem, namely, why Noah curses Canaan, the son of Ham, for his father's sin, when Ham shamefully dishonours his father (Gen 9:20-25). Brown ingeniously suggests that in his drunken confusion, Noah "spluttered the name of the wrong son, the one that was always on his mind ever since he drowned".[19] Therefore, this textual discrepancy between the Bible and the Qur'an, rather than being a cause for submitting to the authority of one over the other, rather "provides an instance where knowledge of the Qur'an resolves a textual conundrum in the biblical text…it is becoming increasingly

---

[19] Brown, *Noah's Other Son*, 52.

obvious that understanding of the Bible can be dramatically enhanced by knowledge of the Qur'an."[20]

What are we to say to this? Firstly, it is hermeneutically absurd to suggest that the plain meaning of a text is inaccessible for as much as two thousand years and awaits the writing of another book. Certainly, Biblical interpreters affirm that the New Testament provides the interpretive key to the Old Testament, but in affirming this they are not suggesting that the text, as it stands, made no sense to the original readers.

Why was Canaan cursed? There is no indication in the narrative that he, in anyway, participated in his father's dishonourable act. As Kenneth Mathews reminds us, Hebrew theology recognised that due to parental influences future generations usually committed the same acts as their fathers, whether good or bad. And, certainly in this case, Israel's future history bore this out.[21] If Shem's descendent, Abraham became the father of Israel, Ham's descendent, Canaan, became the father of a nation that became notorious for its sexual depravity, and remained a constant thorn in the side of God's people.

Finally, a few observations need to be made about Brown's attempts to reconcile the Bible's and the Qur'an's respective teachings on the person of Christ and the Trinity, and his assessment of Muhammad. Of course, Brown knows both his topic (who Jesus is) and his dialogue partners (the Jew and the Muslim) too well to suggest there can ever be anything like agreement on the identity of Christ. The most he hopes for is some common ground; "the possibility of a new understanding of each other".[22] Intriguingly, Brown finds this common ground in *The Gospel of Thomas*, which "might be seen as a gospel with a different slant, rather than a different gospel". While acknowledging that the Jesus of this non-canonical gospel works no miracles and makes no atonement for sins, he tentatively suggests that the "Jesus Lite" of this 'gospel' and the Qur'an may have some appeal to Jews, Muslims and disenchanted Christians. At the same time, Brown is

---

[20] Brown, *Noah's Other Son*, 53.

[21] Kenneth A. Mathews, *Genesis 1:1-11:26* (Nashville: Broadman & Holman, 1996), 421.

[22] Brown, *Noah's Other Son*, 187.

aware that such a proposal, which compromises the Christian understanding of salvation, is too high a price to pay. How then, can he maintain orthodoxy in his understanding of the person and work of Christ, with openness to the genuineness of the Qur'an as a revelation from God and the inclusion of Jews and Muslims in the saved people of God?

His answer is found in, what he calls, the 'I AM principle'. Brown, like many who hold an inclusive view of salvation, is uncomfortable with interpretations of the "I AM" statements which suggest they contain an implicit or explicit claim to uniqueness, particularly as expressed in a restrictivist view of salvation. Rather, Brown suggests, "Jesus spoke as the Cosmic Christ, the Eternal Essence that is in all of us..."[23] So, John 14:6 is reinterpreted to say, "Nobody comes to the Father except through the life giving experience of I AM".[24] It is, therefore, not a claim by Jesus to be the exclusive channel of salvation, rather that he is the bearer of 'the I AM experience' that Abraham and Moses encountered, and that Muhammad bore witness to. In terms reminiscent of Karl Rahner's 'Anonymous Christians', Brown, without denying the Jesus of history, is keen to advocate the 'cosmic Christ', "who is present everywhere God is recognised", and is present in the hearts even of those who deny his divinity and saving work.[25]

Of course, in his desire to extend God's salvation to confessing Muslims and Jews, Brown's work stands firmly in the liberal tradition of Christian inclusivism. His highly selective and sanitized account of the life of Muhammad bears little similarity to the portrayal offered by Stephens. Further, his desire to see Christians accept the Qur'an both as a genuine Scripture sent from God and, in part, a supplement or corrective to some parts of the Bible, will leave many unconvinced.

It is difficult to see how this book will further the dialogue between Muslims and Christians. Liberals from both traditions already have little problem reaching positions of compromise on a range of

---

[23] Brown, *Noah's Other Son*, 198.

[24] Brown, *Noah's Other Son*, 198

[25] Brown, *Noah's Other Son*, 200.

issues. It is not them he needs to convince. It is the conservatives on both sides who are not amicable to theological compromise. For Orthodox Muslims the Bible is a corrupted text and in many contexts, even the possession of the Bible is a mark of apostasy. For such conservatives, any suggestion that Jesus is more than a prophet is *shirk,* the worst form of blasphemy and idolatry. For conservative Christians, while dialogue should be marked by courtesy, civility and a desire for mutual understanding, the price Brown is prepared to pay in his view of Scripture, and the person and work of Christ is far too high.

3. Claiming Abraham: Reading the Bible and the Qur'an Side by Side

Like *Noah's Other Son,* Michael Lodahl's *Claiming Abraham,* has been written in the wake of 9/11 and the apparent escalating tension between Islam and Christianity. Indeed, as I write this section the lead article in today's news is the death of 28 Coptic Christians in Cairo, following the burning of a church and the heavy-handed break-up by the Muslim-dominated army of Egypt of a peaceful Christian demonstration. "We are tired of turning the other cheek", said one angry and grieving Copt. Of course, a similar story could be told on almost any day of the year. For that reason Lodahl begins his plea for mutual understanding with an impassioned plea from a Buddhist: "you People of the Book better get along and get to know each other some time soon".[26]

For Lodahl, like Brown, a great deal is at stake. A mutually sympathetic Christian-Muslim conversation is imperative because, "it appears that the future of our world, at least humanly speaking, may well hang in the balance...the pressure is on. It is incumbent..."[27] In fact, for Lodahl the events of 9/11 were the impetus for his reading, for the first time, the Qur'an. In many ways, this book follows the same format as *Noah's Other Son.* Following the narrative history of the Bible, it compares the teaching of the two sacred texts on many of the key events and characters, Adam, Cain and Abel, Noah, Moses, Mary, and Jesus.

---

[26] Michael Lodahl, *Claiming Abraham: Reading the Bible and the Qur'an Side by Side* (Grand Rapids: Baker, 2010), 1.

[27] Lodahl, *Claiming Abraham,* 2.

Once again, we cannot examine in any detail each comparison this book provides. Therefore, as with *Noah's Other Son*, we will just focus primarily on the book's analysis of the Noah story as it appears in the Bible and the Qur'an, and then make some brief comments on Lodahl's comparative analysis of the presentation of Jesus in the two sacred texts.

The Story of Noah

Turning first to the Bible's and the Qur'an's respective presentations of the story of Noah, whereas Brian Arthur Brown focuses on the question of the identity of Canaan, 'Noah's other son', presumably to demonstrate the complementarity of the Bible and the Qur'an, Lodahl chooses to address the issue which is both the most striking contrast between the two accounts, and by far the one with the most theological significance, namely the contrasting presentations of God. Lodahl discusses the question of God's grief over the sinfulness of humankind, and his regret at having to wipe them out. He rightly acknowledges that, for Muslims, any suggestion that God might be sorry for a decision he has made diminishes God's sovereignty and transcendence and would amount to a culpable betrayal of God rather than a faithful portrayal.[28] Indeed, not only does the Allah of the Qur'an not grieve over the wickedness of his people, he commands Noah himself not to grieve. While Lodahl himself finds this anthropomorphism difficult to reconcile with a God who is omniscient[29], nevertheless he expresses a personal preference for the God of the Genesis account. Indeed, this appears to be his approach to the comparison of the Bible and Qur'an generally. It seems to be more of a question of which holy book better resonates with him personally, than which is true and which is false. For example, in his discussion of the story of Adam, Lodahl expresses a clear preference for the Biblical account. When "pressed to choose" he finds it more amenable to his perception of the role of humanity in the world. But this is Lodahl's preference. He continues, "I must reiterate that, from my perspective, the above scenario should not – or at least need not – be seen as dismissing the

---

[28] Lodahl, *Claiming Abraham*, 115.

[29] This is just one of a number of examples in the book of Lodahl's commitment to Open Theism, the view that God does not know the future and, therefore, cannot, impact the future e.g. 100-101.

Qur'an or denying its revelatory potential".[30] From the very beginning, Lodahl began his study with an openness to the question of the Qur'an's status as a revelatory text. The Qur'an's account of the Cain and Abel story has "the ring of revelation".[31] While conceding that at some points, say in its rejection of the incarnation, "we must finally judge Muhammad's proclamation to be found wanting", Lodahl is clearly loathe to dismiss the Qur'an as a false revelation.

What are we to make of the divergent presentations, not only of God but also Noah himself, in the respective accounts? This is how the Qur'an reports the story of Noah and the Flood:

> Long ago, We sent forth Noah to his people. He said: 'Serve God, my people, for you have no god but Him. Beware the torment of a fateful day.'
>
> But the elders of his people said: 'We can see that you are in palpable error'.
>
> 'I am not in error my people,' he replied. 'I am sent forth by the Lord of the Universe to make known to you my Lord's will and to give you friendly counsel, for I know of God what you know not. Do you think it strange that an admonition should come to you from your Lord through a mortal like yourselves, and that he should warn you, so that you may keep from evil and be shown mercy?'
>
> They did not believe him. So We saved him and all who were with him in the Ark, and drowned those that denied Our revelations. Surely they were blind men. (7.59-64)

In fact, on no less than seven occasions the Qur'an reports the story of Noah, and the stories are all the same: Noah is sent by God to preach to his sinful people, but they reject him because he is just a mortal like them. They say that he is inventing all the revelations he purports to be bringing from God, and they call him a madman. God, then, tells Noah not to worry for he will destroy the evildoers, in part, as a recompense for Noah whom they refused to believe. So, Noah builds the ark, and the people pass by and jeer at him. But Noah said, "If you mock us, we shall mock you just as you

---

[30] Lodahl, *Claiming Abraham*, 115.

[30] Lodahl, *Claiming Abraham*, 90.

[31] Lodahl, *Claiming Abraham*, 111.

mock us. You shall know who will be seized by a scourge that shall disgrace him, and be smitten by a scourge everlasting." The account then records the coming of the animals into the ark, and the drowning of Noah's son.

There are, as we have seen, historical details that differ between this and the biblical account but, as Lodahl rightly points out, the real difference is in the presentation of God. The Genesis account records,

> The Lord saw how great man's wickedness on the earth had become, and that every inclination of the thoughts of his heart was only evil all the time. The Lord was grieved that he had made man on the earth, and his heart was filled with pain. So the Lord said, 'I will wipe mankind, whom I have created, from the face of the earth – men and animals, and creatures that move along the ground, and birds of the air – for I am grieved that I have made them". But Noah found favour in the eyes of the Lord. (Genesis 6:5-8 NIV)

This is one of the Bible's most devastating descriptions and analyses of the human condition. Strikingly, in the biblical account Noah is silent. In fact, in a lengthy three-chapter description of the flood the biblical Noah doesn't say a word; he's not the focus of the story. By contrast the Quranic accounts are records of Noah's conversations either with God, or the people of his generation. To quote Lodahl, the Quranic Noah is 'noisy'. And most of the conversations deal with the attacks of the unbelievers on Noah himself, and his continued self-justifications. It is somewhat remarkable that neither Brown nor Lodahl recognise the striking similarity between the attacks levelled on Noah (and, indeed, most of the prophets in the Qur'an) and the sort of attacks Muhammad suffered from his opponents hundreds of years later, when the people of Mecca called him a madman and rejected his warnings.

But, as Lodahl notes, it is in the portrayal of God that we see the most striking difference: "And the Lord was sorry that he had made man on the earth, and it grieved him to his heart. So he said, 'I will blot them out...'" Words like that from the Bible, could never be written of Allah. In the Qur'an, Noah warns the unbelievers: "God will bring it down upon you *when he pleases*...my counsel will not profit you *if God seeks to lead you astray.*" The God of Islam would never respond to the sinfulness of people the way the God of Noah does, or the God of Jesus Christ. God saw the sinfulness of people and it broke his heart. On no less than three occasions the writer describes how God *felt* about the wickedness of the people he had made. The Lord was grieved that he had made man and the conduct of his creatures deeply pained him. While Lodahl is certainly right that we are dealing here with anthropomorphisms, this is not to suggest that God is devoid of emotion. While God's emotions are, of course, of quite a different order to human emotions, nevertheless they are analogous. So, "after a divine manner", God grieves over the state of mankind. The grief of God here is real grief; it is a bitter, indignation that pains the heart of God.

Fundamentally, this is because the God of the Bible is a personal God, who responds and engages with his people. Further, in the light of the Bible's complete revelation, the Christian would say that we know all this is true because this God took on human flesh and came amongst us in the person of Jesus. On one occasion he looked upon the city of Jerusalem, a city that had persistently rejected, abused and killed the prophets, and would shortly kill him also. And Jesus, like the Lord in Genesis 6, pronounced righteous judgment on this city. He described how it would be crushed to the ground, and how men, women and children would also be crushed, with not one stone left on another. And we are told by the Gospel writers that as Jesus uttered this terrible judgment, the tears were rolling down his cheeks.

So, in the contrasting analyses of the Noah story we are confronted with differences of much greater theological significance than, how many of Noah's family entered the ark, or a justification for the cursing of Noah's son, we are met with contrasting presentations of God. Quite simply, the presentation of God in the Genesis account (let alone in the Gospels) is so different from the God of the Qur'an, that Muslims would find the Biblical presentation offensive and blasphemous.

The Story of Jesus

Once again, we will just make a few remarks about Lodahl's comparative analysis of the Bible and the Quran's presentation of Jesus. Like *Noah's Other Son, Claiming Abraham* is marked by a generous, irenic spirit. Lodahl has no desire to exaggerate the differences between the contrasting accounts, and this is as true of his comparative treatment of Jesus, as any other prophet. Positively, he affirms that there is more common ground between the two books than many people realise. In particular, the recognition of Jesus as a miracle worker, and in the role he will play in the age to come. At the same time "we cannot minimise the differences or, in the interest of peaceability with Islam, jettison the church's historical testimony and traditional confessions regarding Jesus as the Messiah, God's uniquely and supremely Anointed One, "the Son of the Living God" (Matt 16:16).[32]

In particular, Lodahl investigates the two greatest issues that divide Islam and Christianity: the person of Jesus, and the contrasting accounts of his crucifixion. While not conceding the Qur'an's highly minimalistic presentation of the identity of Jesus as no more than a prophet, Lodahl points out that the Qur'an's presentation reminds Christians not to speak of Christ's divinity too imprecisely. While it is true that the Messiah is God, it would be incorrect to say that God is the Messiah: "Jesus does not simply equal God, pure and simple without remainder."[33] With respect to Islam's general denial of Christ's crucifixion Lodahl rightly, I believe, sees that the issue, for Muslims, is that God would not allow such a righteous prophet to suffer and die so shamefully. Allah always vindicates his faithful prophets. He cannot allow those who oppose and insult his servants the final victory.

Lodahl's conclusion, rightly, is that "in mainstream traditional Islam there is only Jesus the great prophet, 'peace be upon him', who was delivered from an awful and humiliating death by the superior planning and power of God."[34] Once again, as we saw with the Quran's presentation of Noah, I would add that there is an apologetic agenda behind the Qur'an's picture of Jesus. Chiefly he is presented to vindicate Muhammad's own apostleship. The Qur'an emphasises the opposition of the Jews to Christ, from the moment of his conception to his final hour. This is presented to demonstrate the veracity of Muhammad's claim to apostleship, as he too encountered similar calumny, ridicule, and rejection. Yet, God vindicated Muhammad, and he returned triumphant to Mecca.

---

[32] Lodahl, *Claiming Abraham*, 150.

[33] Lodahl, *Claiming Abraham*, 152.

[34] Lodahl, *Claiming Abraham*, 162.

Both Brown and Lodahl rightly recognise that in the Qur'an Christ is admired, esteemed, and respected. He is a faithful prophet, a great wonder worker, and a man who brought a true revelation from God. However, what both books fail to really make clear is that, for Muslims, the Christ of the Qur'an, Isa, is not to be confused with the Christ of the New Testament. According to Muslim apologetics the New Testament Christ is a concoction of others, notably the Jewish renegade and false prophet, Paul. In Muslim apologetics the Christ who is divine and who saves the world by his atoning death is a Pauline invention, which later influenced the spurious accounts of Christ's life penned by his so-called biographers, Matthew, Mark, Luke and John. The historical Christ, who preached the gospel of Jesus, which is Islam, has sadly been lost to history, and all that can reliably be recovered about him is to be found in the Qur'an and Muslim tradition. In the end, a neutral observer must decide between these two Christs, for they are incompatible and opposed to each other.

In his classic work, *The Muslim Christ*, Samuel Zwemer writes, "Christ has a place in Islam as one of the greater Prophets, and that the Koran gives precious glimpses of the Messiah's greatness, but yet falls short of unveiling his glorious perfection and Divine majesty. Mohammad leads his followers to the portal, but he fails to open the door."[35]

Zwemer argues, convincingly, that in Islam Muhammad is the Muslim Christ. He is the object of reverence and obedience. But it is not just that Islam supplants Christ with Muhammad, it actually defines itself over and against Christ. The denial of the incarnation, the atonement, and the resurrection of Jesus, the cardinal Christian affirmations about Jesus are an important part of Islamic belief, and are regularly expounded from the pulpits of mosques, and are readily available in the writings that emanate from Islamic publishing houses. The average Christian will grow up in a Christian home totally ignorant of Islam and Muhammad. The average Muslim will grow up knowing with a surety that Muhammad is the prophet of God, and Christ is not the Son, is not the Saviour of the world, and did not die on a cross and rise again.

---

[35] Samuel Zwemer, *The Muslim Christ*. www.truthnet.org/Islam/MuslimChrist.

In other words, we must never underestimate the magnitude of the challenge of bringing about in Islam a more conciliatory approach to the Bible and to Jesus.

Conclusion

The Importance of Informed Dialogue

Both Brown and Lodahl are writing in a context where relationships between Christians (or, indeed, non-Muslim people generally) and Muslims are strained. This is nothing new, of course, in the history of the two religions, but with the potential of both sides to access and use weapons capable of a degree of destruction only dreamt of in Tom Clancy novels, the stakes have never been higher. It should also be noted, that this tension may be felt more acutely in the United States than, say, Australia, since the U.S. has been the victim of the greatest attack by Muslim jihadists, and continues to bear a high cost both financially, and in terms of human life, of those involved in the war on terrorism. Both authors are, understandably, keen to lower the temperature of the rhetoric between Christians and Muslims and, rightly, recognise that the best foundation for a growth in mutual understanding is, on both sides, honest engagement with each other's sacred texts.

Most Christians and Muslims are woefully ignorant of the content of each other's holy books (indeed, one could add that both Christians and Muslims today are woefully ignorant of the content of *their own* holy books). Therefore, any attempt to encourage people on both sides to read each other's books is to be warmly commended.

At the same time, both these books, *Noah's Other Son* and *Claiming Abraham* demonstrate the degree to which we approach the books we read with our own prejudices and presuppositions. When one compares the conclusions that William Stephens in the late 19th century makes about the Qur'an ("insufferably dull", "incoherent", "monotonous") and Brian Arthur Brown's conclusions in the early 21st century ("in truth, Islam is beautiful)") then we see how much our prior commitments determine our final conclusions. Nevertheless, dialogue must begin from a basis of knowledge not ignorance.

I would also add that this dialogue needs to be honest dialogue. There is little to be gained by putting the kindest possible interpretation on a given text. Dialogue can be frank and honest without being disrespectful. Both sides need to be willing to give and receive critical challenges from the other about their sacred writings.

How Successful Will These Books Be?

Michael Lodahl begins his book with a plea from a Buddhist for Christians and Muslims to begin to get along. Of course, in the majority of cases individual Christians and Muslims get along just fine. I spent 11 years in the Islamic Republic of Pakistan and cannot recall anything but the most cordial relationships with my Muslim neighbours – and the same was true of all my missionary co-workers. The issue, of course, is the escalating violence being perpetrated by jihadist Muslims who find in their sacred texts, and in the life and example of their prophet, both the model and the mandate for violence against the perceived enemies of Islam. At the same time, it must be acknowledged that in most instances the targets and victims of these violent attacks are other Muslims.

Ultimately, the aim of both of these books is to contribute to a change of perception on both sides about the other. In Brown's book in particular, the aim appears to be the recognition, by both Christian and Muslim, that the two faiths share far more points of commonality than difference. There is a deep and essential unity between the Qur'an and the Bible. Both faiths spring from the same Abrahamic root. Indeed, with varying degrees of confidence both writers wish to concede prophetic status to Muhammad, and revelatory status to both the Bible and the Qur'an. It is their hope, then, that this growth in mutual understanding and appreciation will contribute, albeit in a small way, to putting a halt to the acts of violence that seem to be escalating, especially in the name of Islam. It was, after all, 9/11, the most horrendous of these acts of violence, that prompted the writing of both these books.

The problem, though, with both books is that the kind of people who will read them – or who would agree to take the pulpit in Brian Brown's church – are not the sort of people who need to be convinced. Leaving aside the fact that many conservative Christian students of Islam and the Qur'an will remain unconvinced by the kind of sympathetic analysis that marks Brown's study, and even to a lesser degree, Lodahl's, how would traditional, conservative Muslims view such a study? From my contact with Muslims, it would seem that only moderates would even permit the kind of comparative study undertaken by Brown and Lodahl. For deeply conservative Muslims it demeans the perfect, eternal Qur'an to study it, on an equal basis, alongside a corrupted text.

But now we come to the heart of the problem. Many who read the Qur'an and the hadiths (the voluminous record of the other authoritative words of Muhammad), and study Muhammad's life, conclude that the jihadists are closer to the spirit of true Islam than those who take a more liberal or modernist approach. While some of the statements in the Qur'an about holy war may be ambiguous and contradictory, when one also reads the hadiths and examine the actions of Muhammad after his flight to Medina, it is clear why jihadists find the inspiration for their acts of violence in the person of Muhammad himself, and why they have only contempt for other Muslims who do not join them in the aggressive expansion of Islam and the humiliation of its enemies.[36] In short, the first problem facing contemporary students of Islam and Christianity is to persuade moderate Muslims to examine their own sacred texts critically and honestly. While they continue to affirm that the sacred texts of Islam, and the biographies of the life of Muhammad, present a man of peace and gentleness who'd showed respect to those who opposed him, then it is hard to see how conservatives on either side will accord them any credibility. But then, secondly, these Muslim moderates will need to convince the radical conservatives that the conservative hermeneutic they adopt in their reading of the Qur'an is fundamentally flawed. In other words, they will need to convince the deeply conservative scholars that the correct hermeneutic for interpreting the Qur'an is a contextualized one; that is, a hermeneutic that extracts principles from the Qur'an which are appropriate for the 21st century and consistent with living in a religiously and politically pluralistic world. If Muslims and Christians are a dysfunctional family, as Brown colourfully describes the relationship, the real challenge is not convincing the peaceful cousins to keep talking to each other, but to persuade the troublesome black sheep (the jihadist) to come back into the fold. Noble as the goals are of *Noah's Other Son* and *Claiming Abraham*, the challenge facing those who are calling for a fresh reading and

---

[36] For a comparative study of holy war in Islam and Christianity see Michael Raiter, *Contending for God in Islam and Christianity* (Lilydale: Bible College of Victoria, 2002).

understanding of the holy books is far greater, and far more difficult, than either writer seems to appreciate. But in this respect, Brown and Lodahl are right: the potential consequences of not bringing about a different reading – especially of the Qur'an – could not be more serious.

The History of Modern Islamophobia

Anthony McRoy

Introduction

It is uncertain when the phrase 'Islamophobia' originated, or who actually coined it, but it seems to have emerged in the late 1980s, and certainly by that time Muslims in Britain were beginning to use that term. In 1997 the Runnymede Trust produced a report on the phenomenon called *Islamophobia - a challenge for us all*. It examined the phenomenon of anti-Muslim prejudice and suggested a grid of eight features:

1) Islam seen as monolithic and static rather than as diverse and dynamic;

2) Islam seen as other and separate rather than as similar and interdependent;

3) Islam seen as inferior not different;

4) Islam seen as an enemy not as a partner;

5) Muslims seen as manipulative not as sincere;

6) 'Racial' discrimination against Muslims defended rather than challenged;

7) Muslim criticisms of 'the West' rejected not considered;

8) Anti-Muslim discourse seen as natural not problematic.[1]

We will address the Report in more detail shortly. Islamophobia has now become a staple phrase used in English-speaking countries and beyond. In popular parlance, especially by Muslims, it is seen as equivalent to anti-Semitism, with which it is often compared. Modern Islamophobia has arisen in late twentieth century, largely in aggressively secular European countries, and the essence of its animosity is not that Muslims deny the deity of Christ, but rather that Islam as a religion, or at least certain manifestations thereof, is incompatible with Western *culture* and security. Its expression

---

[1] Runnymede Trust, *Islamophobia: A Challenge for Us All. Report of the Runnymede Trust Commission on British Muslims and Islamophobia* (London: Runnymede Trust, 1997), 4ff.

crosses the political spectrum. For example, right-wing elements view with hostility what they see as the intrusion of Islam into traditional Western culture – for example, halal meat in schools, Islamic dress, the use of Arabic, etc., all of which they see as culturally alien to the West.

In contrast, liberal and left-wing elements object to the very religiosity of Muslims, the fact that women are covered-up, that their rights seem to be inferior to those of men, that homosexuality is roundly condemned, and that halal slaughter is inhumane by Western standards. Across the political spectrum, there are objections to Islamic restrictions on free speech in the name of countering 'blasphemy'. All sides of the spectrum view Islamic involvement in terrorism as a source of anxiety. Further, the fact that Religion and State are not separated in Islam is a major cause of concern, especially given the burgeoning nature of Muslim communities in Western countries through a combination of immigration and high birth rates, and the sometimes expressed desire of Muslims to see the West 'won for Islam'.

We should also distinguish two aspects of Islamophobia. Firstly, cultural criticism of Islamic religious tenets, notably on issues such as women's rights, the rights of minorities, issues relating to apostasy and blasphemy, and concerns about jihad. Secondly, there is antagonism to Muslims themselves, sometimes thinly-hiding ethnic antagonism, such as Far Right animosity to Muslims of Third World (i.e. non-White) heritage, and to the Bosnian Muslims and Kosovar Albanians during the wars that followed the collapse of Yugoslavia. Further, there is antagonism towards Muslims for engaging in acts that threaten life and liberty, such as Jihad in various scenarios, notably 9/11, 7/7, the Bali and Madrid bombings, and attempts by Muslims to prevent the publication of works which they deem as blasphemous.

The Iranian Revolution and *The Satanic Verses* Controversy

Before 1979, the average post-war Westerner knew little about Islam, and so the emergence of Islam as a political force in the 1979 Iranian Revolution was a shock to everyone across the political spectrum, and not just because a popular uprising had removed a Western client-regime. Western secularist tendencies and the concept of the separation of Church and State inevitably contributed to the surprise and anxiety, and also turned the response from one of puzzlement and shock to one of antagonism. Principally, the latter matured as a reaction to the revival of *hudud* punishments by the new regime in Tehran, the jailing and execution of dissidents, and the obliging of women to wear the *chador*, etc. Simply put, the idea of a modern state choosing to become a theocracy was alien to contemporary Western culture. Simultaneous with this were moves towards Islamisation in Pakistan, notably in the fields of *hudud* punishments, the Blasphemy and *Zina* laws, and constitutional discrimination against religious minorities.

However, the main source of hostility arose from the capture of the US Embassy in Tehran by Islamic students in November 1979 and the ensuing hostage crisis lasting until 1981. Islam, in the popular Western mindset, now began to be associated with terrorism and violation of international norms. This was reinforced by the emergence of Hezbollah in Lebanon after 1982, notably its involvement in the 1983 US embassy and the US Marine barracks bombings in Beirut, the latter which brought 'suicide bombings' to the international consciousness. The idea of 'martyrdom' through being the agent of a violent act was, again, alien to contemporary Western culture. Paradoxically, although the Afghan *mujahideen* were armed by the US, their jihad against the USSR and its puppet Communist regime in Kabul also impressed upon Westerners the political and military character of Islam.

It should be recognised that up to the late 1980s, the growing association of Islam with political oppression and violence was seen as something *external* to the West – it happened in places such as the Middle East or Central Asia. The decisive emergence of Islamophobia in the West can be traced back to an event in the UK beginning in 1988 – the controversy surrounding Salman Rushdie's book *The Satanic Verses*. The author, originally from an Indian Muslim background, had used a story about Muhammad being deceived by Satan as the back-drop for his novel, where the main characters have names such as the derogatory Crusader name *Mahound* for Muhammad, the term *Jahiliya,* the 'age of ignorance', for Mecca, the names of the wives of the Prophet for the prostitutes in the city, etc. In the eyes of most Muslims, especially in Britain, where the novel originated, Rushdie was guilty of apostasy and blasphemy, especially the latter: 'it is not the crime of apostasy, but

Shatm al-Rasul (blasphemy against the Prophet) to which Rushdie remains accountable.'[2]

A campaign which began against the book, urging its withdrawal, and including government lobbying and court action, failed. This led to a major miscalculation by the British Muslim community: the infamous burning of the book in Bradford on 14 January 1989, organised by the Bradford Council of Mosques, with young men angrily stamping on the book. This was filmed, and sent to TV stations to be aired with the aim of attracting public attention. However, this spectacularly backfired, with Muslims being compared to the Nazis or the Inquisition for engaging in book-burning.[3] Hostility also came from traditional spheres of support, such as the Community Relations Council and the Commission for Racial Equality (CRE, now subsumed under the Equality and Human Rights Commission) – not least because Rushdie was himself a favoured liberal-left figure:

> The Community Relations Council was caught in a dilemma: Salman Rushdie was respected for his views on anti-racism and his written and video materials were widely used. Moreover *The Satanic Verses* included much material congenial to the left and accessible to an anti-racist constituency. Therefore, the CRC decided to 'adopt no position on the book... [since] the specific issues relating to the concerns of the Muslim community... are of a religious nature...'[4]

Sher Azam of the Bradford Council of Mosques declared that the CRE had 'failed right from the start to understand the Muslim community', and further alleged that they had been used by the Government against 'Muslim aspirations... they have taken the side against the Muslim community.'[5]

The media and general public viewed British Muslims as intolerant fanatics, as implied by the press reaction to the Bradford book-

---

[2] M. M. Ahsan and A.R. Kidwai (ed.), *Sacrilege versus Civility: Muslim Perspectives on the Satanic Verses Affair,* (2nd ed; Leicester: Islamic Foundation, 1993), 57.

[3] Gilles Kepel, *Allah in the West* (Cambridge: Polity Press, 1997), 138.

[4] Philip Lewis, *Islamic Britain* (London: I. B. Tauris, 1994), 160.

[5] 'CRE chief calls to silence "extremists"' in *Muslim News,* No. 17, (July 1990), 1.

burning.⁶ For example, a Senior Citizen sent a letter to the Bradford Council of Mosques, addressed to 'The Muslim Fanatics', which warned them that her husband had not fought in two world wars in vain, implying that he had fought for the very liberty the Muslims were assaulting.⁷ The Muslim campaign was seen as an attack on British traditions of free speech, which united differing ends of the political spectrum against the campaign. This was crucially reinforced when Ayatollah Khomeini delivered his *fatwa* on 14 February 1989 sentencing Rushdie and those associated with the book to death. In Britain, 'many Muslims, especially the young... saw the fatwa as a logical next step after the book-burning.'⁸ Akhtar states that many Muslims 'applauded Khomeini as a hero' for his *fatwa*.⁹

However, the general non-Muslim response was one of horror, that a foreign leader could threaten a British author merely for writing a book, and further shock and disgust that such an action could receive such support from British citizens. Thus, the perceived support of the Muslim community, at least for many within that community, produced a legacy which left non-Muslims in the West with an image of Muslims as violent, not because of a military occupation, as in Lebanon or Afghanistan, or because of political oppression, as in Shahist Iran, but simply because a Western author living in a Western country wrote a book which broke no British laws, but which offended the Islamic religion. Islam – and the Muslim community – was henceforth often seen as a *violent* threat to Western *liberty* in Western countries, as oppose to simply Western policy in Muslim countries. Fully-fledged modern Islamophobia in the West largely dates from this time.

---

⁶ Lewis, *Islamic Britain*, 158.

⁷ Akhtar, Shabbir, *Be Careful with Muhammad!: The Salman Rushdie Affair* (London: Bellew Publishing, 1989), 43.

⁸ Kepel, *Allah in the West*, 140.

⁹ Akhtar, *Be Careful with Muhammad!*, 64.

The Runnymede Trust Report, 9/11 and 7/7

In the years that followed the Rushdie crisis, events such as the first Iraq War, which saw questions raised as to the loyalty of Western Muslims to their state of residence, and then the Bosnian crisis, with its anti-Muslim pogroms, raised the issue of anti-Islamic or anti-Muslim sentiment to the wider public consciousness. In 1997, the highly respected Runnymede Trust, a liberal body, published its report, *Islamophobia – a Challenge to us all*. This enabled the concept and indeed, its nomenclature, to enter the public discourse. In 2000, Derby University in conjunction with the Home Office issued a report on religious discrimination which among other features, examined anti-Muslim attitudes/discrimination.[10] This in effect gave official recognition to the issue.

Other factors have led to deeper awareness of the phenomenon. The rise of Far Right parties across Europe, which have highlighted anti-Muslim hostility in their programmes, has also made the issue a more acute point. In Britain, the British National Party made Islamophobia a feature of its campaigning, notably in elections, such as in Oldham in 2001, with this election leaflet, as reported by a British Muslim group:

> Winning for White Oldham: Winning for You
>
> Crazy, isn't it? Muslim rioters tear the town apart, attacking white people, houses and shops, and petrol-bombing and shooting at the police - and yet whites like us are getting the blame!

It ends:

> Nick Griffin and the BNP, or the pro-Muslim Labour party? Make up your own mind and think of your family as you vote British National Party.[11]

More latterly, the English Defence League has been formed, and engaged in demonstrations against mosques, such as a proposed

---

[10] Paul Weller and Kingsley Purdam, *Religious Discrimination in England and Wales: Interim Report* (London: Derby University/Home Office, 2000).

[11] Ahmed, Nafeez Mosaddeq; Bodi, Faisal; Kazim, Raza & Shadjareh, Massoud, *The Oldham Riots: Discrimination, Deprivation and Communal Tension in the United Kingdom* (London: Islamic Human Rights Commission, 2001), 12.

new mosque in Dudley.[12] In Switzerland, the Swiss People's Party won 62 of the 200 seats in the 2007 Federal election. It was the major force behind the 2009 referendum which resulted in a ban on any further construction of minarets in the country. In the Netherlands, Geert Wilders' Freedom Party became the third largest party in Parliament in the 2010 elections. Wilders is known for his antagonistic comments about Islam, enshrined in his 2008 film *Fitna,* which was widely condemned by leading Muslims around the world.

Even outside the Far Right, liberal-left elements have been accused of pandering to Islamophobia. In the 2010 UK General Election, Oldham Labour MP Phil Woolas was accused by the Muslim Public Affairs Committee (MPAC) of stoking 'racial tensions' between communities.[13] Woolas issued leaflets accusing his Liberal-Democrat opponent, Elwyn Watkins, of trying 'to woo Muslim extremists'.[14] The 2010 US Congressional elections were also affected by a campaign to prevent the construction of a new mosque near Ground Zero in New York, with Senator Harry Reid (Democrat) of Nevada urging that it be built elsewhere, and Republican candidate Elliott Maynard, in West Virginia exclaiming 'Do you think the Muslims would allow a Jewish temple or Christian church to be built in Mecca?'.[15] In the eyes of Muslims, electoral Islamophobia is a frightening reality.

Along the lines of *The Satanic Verses* controversy, Muslims have felt that media/cultural Islamophobia has continued and intensified, as exemplified by Wilders' film *Fitna.* Before that in 2004, Theo van Gogh and politician Ayaan Hirsi Ali produced the film *Submission,* which also was widely condemned by Muslims. The following year

---

[12] 'Police clash with right-wing demonstrators during protest against plans for new mosque' in *Daily Mail,* http://www.dailymail.co.uk/news/article-1263276/English-Defence-League-protesters-clash-police.html#ixzz1DwmbIMsz (3 April, 2010).

[13] MPAC, Disgusting Islamophobia: Woolas Smears *MPACUK* with Fake 'Death Threat' Leaflet, http://www.mpacuk.org/story/040510/woolas-attempts-smear-mpacuk-imaginary-death-threats.html#ixzz17RSrTJJE (2010).

[14] 'Equality Commission Chief Criticises Woolas Leaflets' in *Saddleworth News,* http://www.saddleworthnews.com/?p=2140 (8 June, 2010).

[15] Carl Hulse 'G.O.P. Seizes on Mosque Issue Ahead of Elections', in *New York Times,* http://www.nytimes.com/2010/08/17/us/politics/17mosque.html (16 August, 2010).

the Danish newspaper *Jyllands-Posten* was embroiled in a controversy about its publication of cartoons satirising Muhammad. However, the same features that promoted Islamophobia were present in these crises – i.e. the involvement of repressive, sectarian Muslim regimes, the sense that Muslims were attacking free speech, and also threats of violence, which in the case of van Gogh, led to his assassination. Hence, the Muslim reaction to these events only served to enhance and justify Islamophobia in the eyes of the wider public.

Al-Qaida's 9/11 attacks on the US produced a new wave of anti-Muslim sentiment. The mass murder of around three thousand people caused an outburst of Islamophobic outrage and anger, some of it violent: 'The FBI data suggests a 1,600-percent surge in anti-Islamic hate crimes in the days following the Sept. 11 attacks. The research also found a similar increase in hate crimes against people who may have been perceived as members of Islam, Arabs and others thought to be of Middle Eastern origin.'[16] There were also hate crimes in various Western countries, sometimes misconstruing Sikhs for Muslims. This was despite near-universal condemnation from US and other Western Muslim organisations, and from the Muslim states. The attacks led to an upsurge in articles, programmes and books about Islam, some of them obviously polemical, usually taking Huntingdon- style 'Clash of Civilisations' approach, and presenting Al-Qaida as a valid expression of Jihad and indeed Islam. Perhaps the most obvious expression of this populist Islamophobia is the bumper stick available in America and Britain which reads: *'I learned All I Need To Know About Islam On 9/11.'*

This trend accelerated after the Madrid and Bali bombings, but especially after 7/7 – the London bombings on 7 July 2005. Fifty-two people were murdered by this Al-Qaida attack. What set this apart from previous Al-Qaida assaults against Western countries was not its scale –the number of people massacred was obviously lower than those murdered on 9/11 – but rather the identity of its perpetrators. All were British citizens, and all but one actually born in the UK. Britain's worst-ever terrorist incident was carried out by

---

[16] Marc Ransford, 'Many minority groups were victims of hate crimes after 9-11' in *Ball State University Newscenter*, http://www.bsu.edu/news/article/0,1370,-1019-12850,00.html (October 9, 2003).

Britons. This brought to the surface an issue which has caused great concern to Muslims in the West – accusations that they are a 'fifth column', whose loyalty to the country is in question. Linked to this is not only concern about Islamic violence, but rather the idea that Muslims want to replace liberal-democratic traditions of the West with the Shari'ah, at least in stages, leading to full political Islamisation. Various comments by Muslim leaders, the emergence of Islamic financial institutions in the West, and the growth in Islamic schools have aided that anxiety, as have polls, such as one by ICM in 2006 which showed that 40% of UK Muslims support the introduction of Shari'ah in 'areas of Britain which are predominantly Muslim.'[17]

Conclusion

The emergence of modern Islamophobia since the late 1980s is in effect a reaction to incidents of jihad against Westerners, especially to attacks carried-out in Western countries, and to the clash of cultures between Muslims and Western liberal traditions regarding personal liberty. This is demonstrable from an analysis of the historical record. It is true that anti-Muslim extremists have exploited tensions rising out of these events, but with few exceptions (e.g. the Bosnian crisis, where innocent Muslims were massacred), Islamophobia is clearly *responsive* in nature, specifically a reaction to Islamic violence and attacks on democratic liberties, notably free speech. Had there been no Iran Embassy hostages; no *Satanic Verses* controversy; no attempts to censor the media for 'blasphemy', as with the Danish cartoons; no 9/11 and 7/7; and no demands for the territorial imposition of Shari'ah in the West, there would have been little anti-Muslim sentiment, at least outside Far Right elements. The implications for combating Islamophobia are therefore surely obvious.

---

[17] Muslims Poll, ICM, http://www.icmresearch.co.uk/pdfs/2006_february_sunday_telegraph_muslims_poll.pdf#search="sharia" (February 2006).

An Exegetical Study of the Qur'anic Teachings on the Jewish People

Jannah Walters

The purpose of this paper is to take a look at a sampling of passages from the Qur'an regarding the Jewish people. While a broader Scripture-wide survey would be incredibly helpful, due to the confines of this paper, I have narrowed the scope of study to Sura 21 and Sura 2. These two suras offer a reasonable sampling of the Qur'anic teaching on the Jews – each from its respective time period. Furthermore, they are taken from opposite ends of the Qur'an's revelatory chronology: Sura 21 from the First Meccan Period, and Sura 2 from the Medinan Period.

Setting the Stage

Historical Context

It must always be remembered that Muhammad received the revelations comprising the 114 suras of the Qur'an over a period of 23-years. These years saw numerous changes and transitions, as the faith now known as Islam developed and came into its own. The earlier revelations were given while Muhammad and his followers were still in Mecca – weak, vulnerable, and constantly facing the threat of extinction. The revelations continued through the religious group's migration to Medina, through the struggles of the Medinan Ummah, through the rise of political and military power, and eventually through their triumphant return to Mecca as a conquering faith – emancipated and unique among the monotheistic traditions.

These 23 years marked events and transitions which are staggering in light of their continuing historical significance. Moreover, they provide the framework for and oftentimes the explanation of the collective suras which comprise the Qur'an. The former Muslim professor of history and culture at Al-Azhar University, Mark Gabriel, explains that the process of revelation was "often directly related to what was occurring in Muhammad's life at the time."[1]

---

[1] Mark A. Gabriel, *Islam and the Jews* (Lake Mary, FL; FrontLin, 2003), 45.

Many texts otherwise opaque in meaning, become substantially more lucid when the historical backdrop is consulted. Muhammad's relationship with the Jews saw a marked shift between the Meccan and Medinan periods. While he obviously had some familiarity with Jewish tradition while in Mecca, it is unclear the nature and extent of his interaction with the Jews before the time of the Hijra.[2]

The Doctrine of Abrogation

For the Muslim and non-Muslim alike, making sense of Qur'anic attitudes and teachings on the Jewish people can be a baffling process. While some passages seem to imply a rather tolerant view of Jews and their religion, others seem to negate such sentiments in calls for disdain if not outright violence. Of course, there is no shortage of Muslim movements utilizing select portions of Qur'anic scripture to validate their own social agendas and/or theological ideologies – whether that of war, peace, or anything in between.

The widely accepted approach to apparent disparity within the Qur'an is that of *abrogation*: Sura 2:106 says, "Any revelation We cause to be superseded or forgotten, We replace with something better or similar."[3] In other words "when there is a contradiction between two verses in the Qur'an, the newer revelation overrides the previous [one]."[4] Apparently this widely accepted practice among Muslims of both Sunni and Shia traditions is no novel innovation of the modern age:

> "From the earliest centuries of Islam, the jurists and scholars of religious law developed a particular sensitivity for chronological inconsistencies affecting a variety of legal stipulations in the Qur'an. Acknowledging the differences and variations of revelation found in disparate verses of the Qur'an, they developed a theory of abrogation,

---

[2] Sahaja Carimokam, *Muhammad and the People of the Book* (USA: Xlibris Corporations, 2010), 64.

[3] M.A.S. Abdel Haleem, *The Qur'an* (New York: Oxford University Press Inc., 2010), Q. 2:106.

[4] Gabriel, *Islam and the Jews*, 47.

which established lists of abrogating and abrogated verses on the basis of their chronological order."⁵

A Working Chronology

With the doctrine of abrogation in mind, it becomes crucial to have a working understanding of the order in which the revelations were received. While none of the chronological dating systems developed thus far have been universally accepted, the schema developed by the German scholar, Theodor Noldeke, has served as perhaps the most intellectually satisfying approach, and has established a working "rule of thumb for the approximate order of the suras in their chronological sequence."⁶ This schema divides the suras into four historic periods in which they were revealed in the lifetime of Muhammad. These are the First, Second, and Third Meccan Periods, and the Medinan Period.

The Text

As we move through Suras 21 and 2, we will be consulting two key Islamic commentators to act as guides into the Muslim understanding of these passages. First, we will hear from Ibn Abbas, a uniquely authoritative commentator for his close companionship and kinship with The Prophet. Second, we will consult the widely respected 14th century commentator, Ibn Kathir, whose massive work draws upon many traditional Muslim thinkers in addition to Hadith and Qur'anic cross-references.

Sura 21: The Prophets

This sura, indicative in many ways of the Qur'anic literature of the three Meccan periods, is undoubtedly written primarily to the "People of Mecca." It is a warning of coming judgment and a call to forsake idolatry and return to the one, true God. Although the Jews are mentioned very few times directly, the manner in which Muhammad refers to them along with the extent to which he draws upon their tradition is quite telling. During this period it appears that Muhammad viewed both the Jews and Christians as "religious

---

⁵ Gerhard Böwering, 'Chronology and the Qur'ān' in *Encyclopaedia of the Qur'ān* (Georgetown University, Washington DC: Brill, 2011). Brill Online. Columbia International University. http://brillonline.nl/subscriber/entry?entry=q3_COM-00034 (23 November, 2011).

⁶ Gerhard Böwering, 'Chronology and the Qur'ān',
http://brillonline.nl/subscriber/entry?entry=q3_COM-00034

allies" – fellow monotheists backing his theological claims in a world of polytheistic paganism.

The term "Jew" is seldom used during this time, more common are indirect references to people who possess the Scriptures, or historical references to "The Children of Israel." One of the most common ways in which Muhammad references the Jews is in his citation of their Scriptures. Contending with the Meccans regarding the legitimacy of his prophetic ministry, Muhammad tells his interlocutors, "If you [disbelievers] do not know, *ask people who know the Scripture.*"[7] According to both Ibn Abbas and Ibn Kathir, these people who Muhammad cites as authoritative are the Jews, Christians, and perhaps other "people of knowledge among the nations."[8]

Furthermore, these "Scriptures" – the Torah and the Gospels[9] – are validated as inspired words of God. Verse 48 says that

> "In the past We [Allah] granted to Moses and Aaron the criterion for judgment, and a Light and a Message for those who would do right."[10]

The word, "criterion," is rendered by many translators and commentators as "Scripture," and refers to the Torah (which was given to Moses and Aaron). Ibn Kathir goes on to refer to these Scriptures as "heavenly books," and describes them as

> "The distinction between truth and falsehood, guidance and misguidance, transgression and the right way, lawful and unlawful, and that which will fill the heart with light, guidance, fear of Allah and repentance."[11]

---

[7] Haleem, *The Qur'an*, Q. 21:7; emphasis added.

[8] Shaykh Safiur-Rahman al-Mubarakpuri et al (eds.), *Tafsir Ibn Kathir* (Abridged), (2nd ed; Riyadh-London-New York: Darusallam, 2003, 10 vols.). http://www.quran4u.com/Tafsir%20Ibn%20Kathir/Index.htm (23 November, 2011).

[9] Ibn Abbas, *Tanwir al-Miqbas min Tafsir Ibn 'Abbas* (Trans. Mokrane Guezzou, Amman, Jordan: Royal Aal al-Bayt Institute for Islamic Thought, 2007), 351.

[10] Yusuf Ali; *The Qur'an*. http://www.cmje.org/religious-texts/quran/verses/021-qmt.php (23 November, 2011).

[11] Al-Mubarakpuri, *Tafsir Ibn Kathir*.

Again in verse 105, Muhammad seems to extend this endorsement of inspiration to the Psalms:

> "Before this We wrote in the Psalms, after the Message given to Moses: My servants the righteous, shall inherit the earth."[12]

This translation is from Yusuf Ali, but apparently there are some differences of opinion among Muslim scholars as to the exact interpretation of the Arabic used here. With Ali, some say that the Psalms and Torah are the Scriptures in view, while others argue that Muhammad is speaking of the Torah, Gospels, and Qur'an.[13] Taking any of these interpretations, however, would attest to the same key point – that is, that Muhammad viewed the earlier Jewish Scriptures as the inspired word of God, and repeatedly cites them as an authoritative validation for his own prophetic ministry.[14] The qualifying criticisms of corruption later alleged by the Prophet against these Scriptures appear to be out of view at this point.

One of the primary ways in which Muhammad used the Scriptures to validate his prophetic ministry was by retelling biblical stories (often in quite variant versions from those of Judeo-Christian tradition) in order to highlight apocalyptic themes – often drawing comparisons between himself and the persecuted prophets of old. Quoting Allah, verse 41 says,

> "Messengers before you [Muhammad] were also ridiculed, but those who mocked them were overwhelmed in the end by the very thing they had mocked.[15]

These types of assertions can be found throughout these parts of the Qur'an, usually in the tone of warning to disbelievers and assurance to the Prophet and his followers. Following this statement in verse 41, Muhammad takes his readers on a tour of various Old Testament figures who, presumably, had suffered beneath such ridicule and mockery, in the end being divinely exonerated. Included in this summary are characters such as Abraham, Moses, Lot, Noah, David, Solomon, Job, Zachariah, and Mary. Lest there

---

[12] Ali, *The Qur'an*.

[13] Al-Mubarakpuri, *Tafsir Ibn Kathir*.

[14] see also Suras 53:36-38, and 87:18-19.

[15] Haleem, *The Qur'an*, Q. 21:41.

be any doubt as to the shared identity which Muhammad felt with these great men of Scripture, he concludes his historical tour with the divine declaration:

> "Verily, this brotherhood of yours is a single brotherhood, and I am your Lord and Cherisher: therefore serve Me and no other."[16]

Or, as translated by Haleem:

"This is your community, one community, and I am your Lord, so serve me."[17] The word here translated "community" or "brotherhood," is rendered by some as "religion,"[18] or "ummah."[19] Thus, is Muhammad's view of his relationship to these biblical characters: "We Prophets are brothers from different mothers and *our religion is one*."[20] In this way, Muhammad both validates and identifies himself with the Jewish history, tradition, Scriptures, and people.

Muhammad does have at least one complaint against the "People of the Book" at this point, however. That is that "they have torn their unity apart,"[21] and have "broken their religion into fragments."[22] Yet, according to Ibn Abbas and Ibn Kathir, this is not necessarily an injunction against the Jewish people specifically, but refers more to the break between the Jews and the Christians.[23] The complaint is not that they are necessarily misled, unbelieving, disobedient, treacherous, or anything of the sort, but that they have allowed the one, true faith to be divided. Concerning this disturbing reality, however, Muhammad is quickly consoled with the assurance that

---

[16] Ali, *The Qur'an*, Q, 21:92.

[17] Haleem, *The Qur'an*, Q. 21:92.

[18] Pickthall, *The Qur'an*. http://www.cmje.org/religious-texts/quran/verses/021-qmt.php (23 November 2011), Ibn Abbas, 360.

[19] Al-Mubarakpuri, *Tafsir Ibn Kathir.*

[20] Al-Mubarakpuri, *Tafsir Ibn Kathir,* emphasis added.

[21] Ali, *The Qur'an*, Q. 21:93.

[22] Ibn Abbas, on Q. 21:92; 360.

[23] Ibn Abbas, and Al-Mubarakpuri, *Tafsir Ibn Kathir.*

"Yet, will they all return to Us [Allah]. Whoever works any act of righteousness and has faith,- His endeavour will not be rejected: We shall record it in his favour."[24]

This rather tolerant sounding statement seems to indicate that Muhammad does not see his own faith in opposition to that of Judaism or Christianity, but in fact believes that he is purporting and proclaiming the same monotheistic faith held by Judeo-Christian communities. The battle lines are drawn not between the Muslim and the Jew, but between the pagan polytheists and the Scripture-holding monotheists.

According to Muhammad, monotheism has been the theme of the prophets since the beginning of divine revelation itself:

"And We sent no messenger before you, O Muhammad, but We inspired him; tell your people that they should say: There is no God save Me (Allah), so worship Me, so declare My divine Oneness."[25]

Furthermore, the people who are acceptable to God are not said to be those who follow Muhammad or convert to Islam, but who "profess Allah's divine Oneness and with whose monotheism Allah is pleased."[26] While it is a bit ambiguous as to whether Muhammad would see the Jews' monotheism as "acceptable," he at least seems to be leaving that option open as a matter of divine sovereignty beyond his own judgment.

The Historical Shift

The differences between Sura 21 and Sura 2 are conspicuous, to say the least. Interestingly, the earlier suras indicate no evidence of dialogue with Jews as they do with the polytheistic Meccans, indicating a probable lack of feedback from Jewish individuals.[27] Muhammad's migration to Medina and his resulting close proximity to Jewish communities (likely for the first time) seemed to introduce a series of paradigm shifts in his view of both the race

---

[24] Ali, *The Qur'an*. Q. 21:94.

[25] Ibn Abbas, on Q. 21:25; 253.

[26] Ibn Abbas, on Q. 21:28; 253.

[27] Carimokam, *Muhammad and the People of the Book*, 167.

and their religion. Up until this time, Muhammad appeared to hold to the following assumptions:

1) That the Jews were, to some degree, reliable and authoritative in regards to divine truth,[28]

2) That the religion of the Jews was essentially the same as his own,[29]

3) That the Jews would readily accept the validity of his revelations and prophethood.[30]

Thus, reflecting on the content thus far, it could easily be concluded that "the overall sentiment of the Qur'an and the historical literature for this period was [at least] not negative to the Jews."[31] The shift that takes place between revelations of the earlier and latter periods is most notable in both its volume and its tone.

Sura 2: The Cow

Rather than being written to the pagan Meccans with the assumed support of the Jewish community, many sections of Sura 2 are written to and against the Jewish people. Replete with the use of historical narratives recounting stories of Abraham, Moses and other major figures of Jewish history, Muhammad progressively builds his case of an idolatrous and unfaithful people. Indictments against "the Jews" or "the Children of Israel" litter the landscape of this 286-verse sura. They are accused of rejecting God's messages (41), mixing the truth with falsehood (42), hiding the truth (42, 90, 140, 142-146, 159), telling the people what is right and forgetting to do it themselves (44), disbelieving the divine message in spite of clear signs and proofs (87), selling their souls (90), being hard-hearted (88), being envious of Muhammad (90), killing God's prophets throughout history (91), being idolatrous (93), clinging to this life (93), throwing away the covenant (99, 101), practicing witchcraft (102), wishing no good upon the Prophet or believers (104), constantly trying to turn believers back to disbelief (109, 120),

---

[28] Q. 21:7, 48.

[29] Q. 16:43-44.

[30] Q. 28:52-53.

[31] Carimokam, *Muhammad and the People of the Book*, 189.

being deceived (135), turning their backs on truth (137), being entrenched in opposition (137), altering God's revealed Word (211), and dissenting over truth due to rivalry (213).

To these Jews, Muhammad also issues a series of warnings. Countless times he calls them to remembrance – to remember the favor and blessing which God poured out on them as a nation (40, 47, 122), to remember the covenant that was made between them and God (93), and to remember the treacherousness of their ancestors and the punishments that followed (63-65). In similar fashion to those warnings previously issued against the Meccans, they are told to beware of the coming Day of Judgment (122, 159-161). If they do not repent, he warns, they will be humiliated (90), rejected by God (88, 161), will receive "wrath upon wrath" (90), and everlasting torment (174). They are warned that their blood-ties to the righteous patriarchs and prophets do not ensure their own eternal reward, for each person will be held responsible for his own righteousness (134, 141). All within the context of calling the Jews to repentance, Muhammad rounds out his litigation with pleas to the Jews to return to God, honor their covenant with Him and not to reject truth (40-46).

It should be noted, however, that while the majority of the Jews may be in view, there are apparently some to whom this harsh language does not apply. Verses 100-101 read:

> "Is it not the case that every time they make a covenant, *some party* among them throw it aside?- Nay, Most of them are faithless. And when there came to them a messenger from Allah, confirming what was with them, a party of the people of the Book threw away the Book of Allah behind their backs, as if it had been something they did not know!"[32]

That Muhammad says "some party" rather than "all," would imply that there are also some who do not "throw aside the covenant." Although it is unclear which Jews belong to this minority, further probing seems to indicate that these may be none other than those Jews who, in fact, become Muslim.

One theme that has proven notoriously ambiguous is that of tolerance and acceptance or else intolerance and hostility towards

---

[32] Ali, *The Qur'an*, Q. 2:100-101, emphasis added.

practicing Jews. Pertaining to this question there are several passages in Sura 2 worth taking a closer look.

"Anyone who does Good will Not Lose Their Reward"

There are several passages which may lead one to believe with the well-known historian, Karen Armstrong, that "Muhammad never asked Jews or Christians to accept Islam unless they particularly wished to do so, because they had received perfectly valid revelations of their own."[33] However, taking a closer look into surrounding *tafsir* and working within the hermeneutic of abrogation, these passages tend to take on a much further developed interpretation. For example, verse 62 says:

> "Those who believe in the Qur'an, and those who follow the Jewish scriptures, and the Christians and the Sabians,- any who believe in Allah and the Last Day, and work righteousness, shall have their reward with their Lord; on them shall be no fear, nor shall they grieve."[34]

While Ibn Abbas appears to interpret this passage at face value, Ibn Kathir makes two points of qualifying clarification: first, this promise no longer applies to the Jews, Christians, and Sabians, but refers only to those of "earlier nations."[35] Furthermore, this verse was later abrogated by Q. 3:85 which says, "Whoever seeks religion other than Islam, it will never be accepted of him, and in the Hereafter he will be one of the losers." Ibn Kathir explains that, taken in context, this verse is saying that *before* the coming of Muhammad, "every person who followed the guidance of his own Prophet was on the correct path...and was saved," but now, "Allah does not accept any deed or work from anyone, unless it conforms to the Law of Muhammad."[36]

Similarly, verses 82 and 112 make claims which, on the surface, appear to be open-minded and tolerant, while explanatory *tafsir* reveal otherwise. Verse 82 says,

---

[33] Karen Armstrong, *Islam: A Short History* (NY: Random House, 2002), 10.

[34] Ali, *The Qur'an*, Q. 2:62.

[35] Al-Mubarakpuri, *Tafsir Ibn Kathir*.

[36] Al-Mubarakpuri, *Tafsir Ibn Kathir*.

> "But those who have faith and work righteousness, they are companions of the Garden: Therein shall they abide forever."[37]

The two key elements here for those who will be rewarded are faith and works of righteousness. Rather than referring to a broad monotheism, however, according to Ibn Abbas this faith refers to a specific belief in "Muhammad and the Qur'an."[38] Ibn Kathir ventures a step further in saying that not only does this *aya* refer only to those who "believe in Allah and His Messenger and…conform with the Islamic Law," but he specifically addresses the religion of the Jews in this way:

> "Whoever believes in what you Jews did not believe in and implements what you refrained from implementing of Muhammad's religion, shall acquire Paradise for eternity."[39]

Again, verse 112 reads,

> "Whoever submits his whole self to Allah and is a doer of good, he will get his reward with the Lord; on such shall be no fear, nor shall they grieve."[40]

In similar form to verse 82, Ibn Kathir quickly does away with any notion that this passage indicates the acceptability of the Jewish religion or otherwise. Seemingly anticipating such a query, Ibn Kathir clarifies:

> "Yes! But whoever submits his face himself to Allah (i.e. follows Allah's religion of Islamic Monotheism) and he is a Muslim."

Quoting a Hadith from Sahih Muslim, Ibn Kathir continues,

> "The good deeds of the priests and rabbis will not be accepted, even if they are sincerely for Allah alone, because these deeds do not conform with the method of the Messenger, who was sent for all mankind."

The fate of these who disbelieve in Muhammad and do not conform to Islamic law will be humiliation and "the hot blazing fire."[41]

---

[37] Ali, *The Qur'an*, Q. 2:82.

[38] Ibn Abbas on Q. 2:82; 14.

[39] Al-Mubarakpuri, *Tafsir Ibn Kathir*.

[40] Ali, *The Qur'an*, Q. 2:112.

"Fight until there is No More Persecution"

Of the most contested and currently relevant themes of the Qur'an is that of jihad, or the struggle of holy war. While some (such as Karen Armstrong) argue for the tolerant character of the religion, others such as Mark Gabriel (the former Muslim university professor) counter that such teachings are nothing more than a ploy "to make Islam look good to Westerners."[42] Let us return to the text - verses 190-193 pose a fascinating case study:

> "Fight in God's cause against those who fight you, but do not overstep the limits: God does not love those who overstep the limits. Kill them wherever you encounter them, and drive them out from where they drove you out, for persecution is more serious than killing. Do not fight them in the Sacred Mosque unless they fight you there. If they do fight you, kill them – this is what such disbelievers deserve – but if they stop, then God is most forgiving and merciful. Fight them until there is no more persecution, and worship is devoted to God. If they cease hostilities, there can be no further hostility, except towards aggressors."[43]

Of course, this passage raises several questions – not the least of which are: What does it mean to "transgress the limits?" And Who are these "aggressors"? Interestingly, Ibn Abbas points us to the historical context in order to understand the passage. He explains that these verses are primarily referring to fighting *within the Sacred Meccan Sanctuary*. Apparently, during the Muslims' pilgrimage to Mecca, there would be some who would attack and persecute the pilgrims.[44] Understandably, there was some hesitancy to commit bloodshed within the Sacred Precinct during such a holy time. Thus, this passage is one which gives permission to fight back "until there is no more persecution." Of the finer points worth noting is Ibn Abbas' definition of *fitnah* (persecution): that is, "associating partners with Allah and worshipping idols."[45] Ibn Kathir echoes

---

[41] Al-Mubarakpuri, *Tafsir Ibn Kathir.*

[42] Gabriel, *Islam and the Jews,* 51.

[43] Haleem, *The Qur'an,* Q. 2:190-193.

[44] Haleem, *The Qur'an,* footnote, 21.

[45] Ibn Abbas, on Q. 2:193; 16.

this interpretation and even includes unbelief as part of that which constitutes persecution. He explains that

> "Since jihad involves killing and shedding the blood of men, Allah indicated that these men are committing disbelief in Allah, associating with Him in the worship and hindering from His path, and this is a much greater evil and more disastrous than killing."[46]

However, while the definition of those engaged in persecution is quite broad (inclusive of anyone committing the Islamic understanding of shirk or unbelief, which would include practicing Jews[47]), the context of this particular passage appears to only reference fighting while on the holy pilgrimage to Mecca. Ibn Kathir even quotes a Hadith which teaches that the Holy Sanctuary has been purified since the time of this revelation, making this specific command to "fight until there is no more persecution" no longer applicable.[48]

Returning, then, to the subject of this paper, this passage appears to only give license to fight and kill those idolaters and disbelievers who infiltrate the Holy Precinct. Of course, that such a concern was being raised in the first place leads one to wonder about the foregoing practices of killing disbelievers outside of the holy month and place before this time. In any case, while later revelations (such as Q.9:5) appear to call for warfare on a global level,[49] here, the scope appears to be limited.

"There is No Compulsion in Religion"

Finally, we come to that oft-quoted passage, which activists and politicians use to purport the tolerant virtues of the Islamic religion:

---

[46] Al-Mubarakpuri, *Tafsir Ibn Kathir*.

[47] See Q. 21:87-88, 93, 166, 109, 120, 137, etc.

[48] Al-Mubarakpuri, *Tafsir Ibn Kathir*.

[49] On Sura 9:5, Ibn Abbas (193-194) says, "Then, when the sacred months have passed....slay the idolaters...wherever ye find them, whether in the Sacred Precinct or outside it, during the sacred months or at any other time, and take them captive, imprison them, and besiege them in their homes, and prepare for them each ambush on every road they tread for trade." And Kathir agrees, "On the earth in general, except for the Sacred Area, for Allah said, and capture them, executing some and keeping some as prisoners...do not wait until you find them. Rather, seek and besiege them in their areas and forts, gather intelligence about them in the various roads and fairways...this way, they will have no choice, but to die or embrace Islam."

> "Let there be no compulsion in religion: truth stands out clear from error: whoever rejects evil and believes in Allah hath grasped the most trustworthy hand-hold that never breaks...Of those who reject faith the patrons are the evil ones: from light they will lead them forth into the depths of darkness. They will be companions of the fire to dwell therein."[50]

Ibn Abbas and Ibn Kathir seem to agree that, rather than being a statement of religious acceptance, this verse functions as a simple statement of fact: that

> "Whoever Allah directs to Islam...will embrace Islam with certainty. Whoever Allah blinds his heart...will not benefit from being forced to embrace Islam."[51]

In other words, in the Muslim view, the truth of Islam is obvious: one cannot be forced to recognize it – either they will know and confess it or they will not. It should be pointed out that this verse does not negate any call to action against such unbelievers, but merely delegitimizes efforts of forcing one to convert against his or her will.

Conclusion

While there are many passages of the Qur'an yet to be examined which would shed greater light on the subject, the above sampling should offer an adequate window into the Qur'anic teachings on the Jewish people. Hopefully, it has become apparent that the Qur'anic material is far from uniform, but, as The Center for Muslim-Jewish Engagement has phrased it, is "ambivalent about the Jews."[52] The revelations were usually oriented around specific historical events, and as the historical surroundings changed, so did the content and tone of the revelations. Because of the Islamic doctrine of abrogation, it is imperative to run earlier Scriptures through the grid of later ones. And, unfortunately in the case of the Jews, the latter revelations are much harsher than the former.

---

[50] Ali, *The Qur'an*, Q. 2:256-257.

[51] Al-Mubarakpuri, *Tafsir Ibn Kathir*.

[52] *Jewish-Muslim Relations*. Center for Muslim-Jewish Engagement. http://cmje.org/articles/jewish-muslim-relations.php (5 October, 2011).

Other Works Consulted

Bostom, Andrew; The Legacy of Islamic Antisemitism: From Sacred Texts to Solemn History. Prometheus Books; Amherst, NY; 2008.

Durie, Mark; The Third Choice: Islam, Dhimmitude and Freedom. Deror Books, USA; 2010.

Esposito, John; Islam: The Straight Path. Oxford University Press, NY; 1991.

Lewis, Bernard, The Jews of Islam. Princeton University Press; Princeton, NJ; 1984.

Australian Islam and the Battered Wife Syndrome

Bernie Power

It was an unusual line of legal defence. In June 2003, Barrister Tony Lewis told the Melbourne County Court that his Turkish client Fadime Cubuk, 26, was obliged to obey her Muslim husband in committing a crime. He cited the Qur'an's teaching that disobedience was "absolutely forbidden" according to their religion and could bring admonishments, withdrawal of sexual favours, and "a light beating." Mrs Cubuk had been thrown out of the marital home before and was scared of her husband. Consequently she handed over $25,000 to pay some-one to burn down Mohammed Cubuk's failing kebab shop in Pascoe Vale in an insurance scam. The fire also extensively damaged two adjacent buildings. Mr Cubuk was sent to jail for four years for the offence. However Judge Bill White suspended the sentence on Mrs Cubuk because she had been following her "family and cultural upbringing" when she helped her husband engage in crime. "The court was told you were raised in a culture and religion requiring you to obey your husband," the judge observed.

The issue of Islamic wife-beating hit the headlines again in Jan 2009. A You-Tube clip showed Melbourne imam Abu Hamza, of the *Islamic Information and Services Network of Australia* (IISNA), addressing a 2003 seminar on "The Keys to a Successful Marriage." He gave instructions on how to beat one's wife. "The beating the Mohammed showed is like the toothbrush that you use to brush your teeth," he said, describing the 1-2 cm diameter *siwak* stick widely used in the Muslim world for dental hygiene. "You are not allowed to bruise them; you are not allowed to make them bleed." Hitting on the face or any obvious place was also forbidden, since her cooperation might later be required: "How can anyone beat his wife as he beats a stallion camel (or a slave) and then sleep with her?" Muhammad had asked.[1] He also said: "A man will not be asked [on the day of Judgment] as to why he beat his wife."[2]

---

[1] Hadith Sahih alBukhari 8:68.

[2] Hadith Abu Dawud no.2142.

In the Qur'an, Allah had sanctioned the use of violence against wives "from whom you fear misconduct." The suggested treatment concluded with: "hit them." (Qur'an 4:34). Most English translations add the word 'lightly', but the original Arabic text does not include this word. Although the former head of the Islamic Council of Victoria, Yasser Soliman, claimed that "The Prophet Mohammad never beat his wife or smacked the children,"[3] he neglected to say *which* wife (Muhammad had eleven) and he also ignored Islamic history. Muhammad's child-wife Aisha (he was 54 and she only 9 years old when he consummated their marriage) reported that when she once left the house without his permission, "he struck me on the chest which caused me pain." (Hadith Sahih Muslim Bk 4 no.2127).

Unfortunately some Muslims have continued this tradition, for they are told: "You have indeed in the Apostle of Allah a beautiful example to follow." (Qur'an 33:21). An Australian friend who lived in a Bangladeshi village related that Friday night was for wife-beating, and the village rang out with the screams of women suffering their weekly punishment. When challenged, the husbands told him: "How can they respect us if we don't beat them?" Anecdotal evidence from police and ambulance officers in Melbourne and Sydney indicate a higher than normal incidence of violence against women in Muslim families. Independent studies have found that 15% of wives in an Iranian city had been beaten,[4] 25% of married women in Syria,[5] 50% of Palestinian wives,[6] and 80-90% of wives in Pakistan.[7] Such is the power of the Qur'an and Islam's Prophet over Muslims that a single verse and a single incident have birthed a widespread culture of wife-beating. Of

---

[3] http://www.dailytelegraph.com.au/news/cleric-rape-beating-ok-for-wives/story-e6freuy9-1111118629144.

[4] Faramarzi, M. et al. 'Prevalence and determinants of intimate partner violence in Babol city, Islamic Republic of Iran', in *Eastern Mediterranean Health Journal* 11/5 & 6 (September 2005) World Health Organization.

[5] http://www.nytimes.com/2006/04/11/world/middleeast/11syria.html?_r=1 (10, April 2010).

[6] Doug Alexander, 'Addressing Violence Against Palestinian Women' in *International Development Research Centre* (June 23, 2000).

[7] Susanna Price, 'Pakistan's rising toll of domestic violence', BBC News (August 24, 2001).

course, as the above figures suggest, not all Muslim husbands beat their wives.

The pathology of domestic violence shows some interesting parallels with the relationship between Australia and Islam.[8] In recent centuries Muslim contact with Australia had been intermittent. The Malay pearl divers of Western Australia and the Afghan cameleers of Central Australia were temporary residents during the late 19th and early 20th centuries, leaving when their industries waned. Like tradesmen, they came, did their job, earned their money, and left. Since World War II, however, the situation has been different. Just as in 595 AD when the wealthy and influential Khadija proposed marriage to her poor but industrious employee Muhammad, likewise Australia has in recent decades invited Muslims to come and live in the household. In both cases, it was a marriage of convenience. The twice-married Khadija was 40 years old and Muhammad was 25. He had lost his parents at a young age, and was brought up by male relatives, spending years herding goats and camels in the desert. This marriage proposal was his chance for acceptance, stability and prosperity, and he took it. Similarly Australia had a wealth of resources, a burgeoning economy, and massive opportunities for export, but an insufficient and now slow-growing and ageing population. The Muslim world has a high birth-rate but its people suffer from war, political instability, corruption, injustice and poverty. Hundreds of thousands leapt at the chance to come and live in the "lucky country."

The vast majority of Muslims in Australia have presented no problem. Enchanted by the peace, affluence and opportunity that Australia offers, many have blossomed. Muslims have become the CEO of Australia's largest bank, members of parliament, top-level sports stars, and found themselves in the rich list of Australia's highest earners. This success has often come at a cost. Most no longer practice their faith – "Only about 30% of Australian Muslims are religiously observant," notes Melbourne media personality Waleed Aly.[9] When I asked about his mosque attendance, a taxi-

---

[8] It was also applied by a Palestinian Christian in relation to his community's connection with Islam, cited in Mark Durie, *The Third Choice* (Deror Books, 2010), 214.

[9] *The Australian*, 9 December 2006.

driver from Turkey laughed: "Are you kidding? That's what we came to Australia to get away from." For most, Islam is only a matter of cultural identity to be checked on the 'Religion' category of their census form.

Other Muslims, however, brought unhelpful baggage from their homelands. In Broken Hill on 1st January, 1915, an Indian and an Afghani Muslim swore allegiance to the Sultan of Turkey and declared jihad on Australia. They opposed Australia's participation in World War I, since Turkey had allied with the Germans. Their commitment to the Islamic *umma* (nation) over-rode any sense of gratitude or affection for the country that had taken them in. These two men gathered a cache of weapons and ammunition and opened fire on a trainload of unarmed picnickers celebrating the New Year's Day holiday, killing four and wounding seven. Both men were later shot dead by the police as they made a last stand on a hill-top.[10]

The history of violence has continued. Since the attacks in New York and Washington in 2001 which killed about 40 Australians and the Bali bombing in 2002 which killed 88 Australians, world-wide terrorist efforts by Muslims have intensified. Islam-watchers have documented over 15,000 deadly attacks by Muslims, including suicide bombings, since 2001.[11] Australia has not been immune from this trend. Currently 17 men are serving time in Australian prisons for terrorist offences and all of them are Muslim. They had a variety of targets such as the AFL Grand Final in Melbourne, the Israeli embassy in Canberra and Australia's only nuclear reactor in Sydney. One man had 12 fire-arms and 11,755 rounds of ammunition. Clearly the intent was a mass slaughter. Fortunately, none have been successful as yet.

Violence is also used to ensure Islam's continued support within its own community. The Melbourne-based *Islamic Information and Support Centre of Australia* (IISCA) states the following on its website: "Apostasy is defined as a Muslim making a statement or performing an action that takes him out of the fold of Islam. The

---

[10] http://www.abc.net.au/gnt/history/Transcripts/s1051016.htm (7 July, 2010).

[11] http://www.thereligionofpeace.com/ (12 April, 2010).

punishment prescribed for it in the Sunnah [Muhammad's example] is execution."[12]

It is this contrast between Islam's normally peaceful and productive engagement with the Australian community on one hand and potentially violent and destructive opposition on the other that makes Islam such an enigma. It is difficult to anticipate which face of Islam will reveal itself in certain situations.

A similar conundrum is faced by a woman living in an abusive relationship. Her male partner is sometimes loving and kind, and at other times cruel and violent. She is unsure what he might do on any particular day. She lives in fear and uncertainty. Yet she remains committed to the relationship, choosing to think the best about him. Melbourne's Mark Durie notes that "[t]he only strategy she is allowed to use to protect herself is to appeal to his good side through soft talk and grateful praise ... She can never confront and challenge his bad side with direct truth."[13] She rationalizes his behaviour by telling herself that, deep down, he is really a good person and it is not his fault. He has current difficulties, she thinks, or a troubled past, and this somehow excuses his brutal deeds.

Similarly Muslims are often given the benefit of the doubt. The former Prime Minister Malcolm Fraser sought to distance Islam from terrorism by saying: "There is a danger that Islam, which is essentially a peaceful religion, will be blamed for the actions of terrorists."[14] In the minds of most observant people, the connection between Islam and terrorism is patently obvious. Most terrorist acts worldwide are carried out in the name of Islam. A Muslim with a backpack in a crowded place yelling 'Allah Akbar' is probably not about to open a country fair. It is hard to de-link Islam and terrorism, as much as we may wish to.

In attempting to assert their peaceful credentials, Muslims sometimes overplay their hand. When the conservative Rev. Jerry Falwell called Muhammad "a violent man, a man of war ... a

---

[12] http://www.islamconveyed.com/pages/index.php?section=Some Islamic Systems&subSection=Crime and Punishment in Islam&id=41 (10 June, 2010).

[13] Mark Durie, *The Third Choice: Islam, Dhimmitude and Freedom* (Deror Books, 2010), 214.

[14] Malcolm Fraser, *Stephen Murray-Smith Memorial Lecture,* State Library of Victoria , Oct 19, 2005. http://www.erc.org.au/just_comments/1132092507.shtml (13 April, 2010).

terrorist", an Iranian cleric called for Falwell's death and a resultant protest in Bombay turned into a riot, resulting in 5 fatalities. Falwell later apologised.[15] Likewise when Pope Benedict quoted a medieval emperor's dictum that everything Muhammad brought was evil "such as his command to spread by the sword the faith he preached", the Muslim response was as violent as it was predictable. Catholic clergy were murdered, churches were burnt, and a Somali cleric called for the Pope to be killed. A French politician called this "Islam kicking an own goal." An internet-posted photo showed a protesting Muslim man with a placard: "Kill those who say Islam is violent." It was probably a joke, but it made its point. A commentator notes: "When cartoons which suggest that Islam is a violent religion are censored because Muslims might react with violence, the serpent has officially swallowed its own tail. The very idea that we must censor any suggestions that Muslims are violent for fear that they might kill us, adequately telegraphs the mental paradoxes and hypocrisies required to enact such a policy. It is not driven by sensitivity or open-mindedness, but by a cloak of self-deception thrown over naked fear."[16]

It is incidents such as these that reveal some of the contradictions within Islam. Fatwas calling for the deaths of Salman Rushdie, the Bangladeshi Taslima Nasreen, the Kurdish writer Mariwan Halabjayi, and many others as well as the assassinations of Theo Van Gogh in Holland and the attempts on the lives of Egyptian Nobel Prize winner Naguib Mahfouz and one of the Danish cartoonists sit oddly and uncomfortably alongside claims that Islam is tolerant and peaceful.

When such inconsistencies are pointed out, Muslims often point the finger back, claiming that they have been provoked. They give a long list of grievances, from the Jewish opposition to Muhammad, to the Crusades (which they won!), to Western colonialism (while conveniently ignoring the even-longer history of Islamic colonialism), to modern day US and Australian foreign policy. The latter has taken a particularly distressing turn, resulting in the arrest of Iranian-born Sheikh Haron in Sydney last year. He had been

---

[15] http://www.religionnewsblog.com/1198.

[16] http://genuinegopmom.blogspot.com/2010/03/is-america-experiencing-battered-wife.html (6 June, 2010).

writing letters to the families of soldiers killed in Afghanistan. To one family, he wrote: "I feel bad that you have lost your son but I don't feel bad that a murderer of innocent civilians has lost his life." Another war-widow received a hand-delivered letter at her husband's funeral accusing him of being a "criminal, ... killer ... and murderer."[17]

The military action of Australian soldiers overseas now becomes a justification for attacking Australian citizens including children. The following exchange, taped by Australian Federal Police in September 2004 between Melbourne's Abdul Nacer Benbrika and Abdullah Merhi, was used in the trial which convicted them both of terrorism offences. They were aiming to plant bombs at AFL venues in response to John Howard's sending of troops to Muslim lands.

Benbrika: *"If they kill our kids we kill (inaudible) little kids."*

Merhi: *"The innocent ones?"*

Benbrika: *"The innocent ones. Because he kills our innocent ones."*

Merhi: *"And we send a message back to 'em."*

Benbrika: *"That's it."*

Merhi: *"Eye, eye for an eye."*

Benbrika: *"So the jihad exists here."*[18]

Jihadists do not discriminate when targeting terrorist attacks. When it was pointed out that the pedestrians in Times Square on May 1st 2010 were not attacking Muslims, Faisal Shahzad justified his placing of the bomb-laden car with ""Well, the [American] people select the government. We consider them all the same."[19]

The tactic of blaming the victim for the criminal's action is a common one with wife-bashing. "You forced me to do this," is often said by a man as he beats a woman. Such overtones were found in the famous 2006 "cat's meat" sermon by the then Grand

---

[17] http://www.dailytelegraph.com.au/news/sick-skeik-allegedly-taunts-diggers-widows-with-vicious-letters/story-e6freuy9-1225789639331.

[18] http://heraldsunonline.com.au/terror/page5.html (27, April 2010).

[19] http://www.danielpipes.org/8536/faisal-shahzad-jihadi-explains-terrorism (2 July, 2010).

Mufti of Australia, Sheikh Taj Uddin alHilali. "If you take out uncovered meat and place it outside on the street, or in the garden or in the park, or in the backyard without a cover, and the cats come and eat it ... whose fault is it, the cats' or the uncovered meat? The uncovered meat is the problem. If she was in her room, in her home, in her hijab, no problem would have occurred."[20] His later references to rape in that speech implied that women are responsible for being raped.

Sometimes women fall for this line of argument and believe that they are the cause of the violence against them. "The battered woman is conditioned to believe that her punishment is her fault, and she should feel grateful to her abusive partner for sparing her ... all the time acknowledging her own guilt."[21] There is a perverted kind of logic in this approach. "This phenomenon is often seen in abuse victims who have to cope with their abuser's enraged violence. By accepting responsibility for being the cause of his anger, they make it seem controllable and predictable. Their coping mechanism is to blame themselves, rather than face the real problem, which is that they live together with a violent and dangerous individual, who will sooner or later kill them. This is the relationship between the West and Islam."[22]

Al-Hilaly more recently tried to justify the actions of Yemeni terrorist Anwar al-Awlaki as "like a virus produced by the body wanting to fight a microbe."[23] The 'microbe' is presumably the West, with its unwarranted and unprovoked attacks on the peaceful and peace-loving House of Islam. Put in this way, al-Awlaki, who inspired Major Nidal Hassan (the Fort Hood massacre) and Umar Farouk Abdulmutallab (the Christmas Day 2009 'underpants' bomber), becomes a powerful germ-attacker seeking to return the body to health and wholeness.

---

[20] http://www.theaustralian.com.au/news/nation/muslim-leader-blames-women-for-sex-attacks/story-e6frg6nf-1111112419114 (7 June, 2010).

[21] Mark Durie, *The Third Choice*, 214.

[22] http://genuinegopmom.blogspot.com/2010/03/is-america-experiencing-battered-wife.html (6 June, 2010).

[23] *The Age* (Melbourne), 15 April, 2010.

Unfortunately many in Australia and elsewhere have begun to accept this discourse. In a radical rewriting of history, the Crusades are presented as a malicious attack on peaceful and progressive Muslim lands. Choudri Mohammed Naim described interfaith dialogues in the US which began with the Christians "denouncing the Crusades, the eighteenth- and nineteenth-century colonial expansions into Islamic lands ... when the "West" (Christianity) encountered the "East" (Islam) and behaved shamefully. The listeners nodded in agreement. One Muslim speaker mentioned the expulsion of the Moors from Spain as another such moment, and all heads were further lowered in sorrow and shame." This University of Chicago professor then states the unstateable: "Amazingly, no one asked how the Moors arrived in Spain in the first place, or what had brought Muslims to the land of the Testaments. It was as if there had been no imperial expansion of Islam, no Arab conquests of Syria, North Africa, and Spain... Islamic history unfolded as a series of conquests... the sword was very much present in the story of Islam's expansion, too."[24]

"Given the choice between blaming the criminal for his crimes, or his victims for having provoked him-- the political and cultural elites of the very countries targeted for terror have chosen to turn the blame inward. They have placed their sordid faith in the belief that the best way to manage Islamic rage, is by relentlessly appeasing and avoiding any provocations that might cause it to flare up."[25] Likewise many in the West, including governments, the media and churches, have sought to stifle any debate about or criticism of Islam for fear of upsetting Muslims and the backlash which may occur. Unfortunately appeasement is rarely successful in such situations. This was recognised long ago by the Jewish physician and philosopher Moses Maimonides (1135-1204). He lived under Islamic rule in Spain but "later moved to Cairo because he would not adopt the Muslim faith."[26] The Jews in Islamic Cordoba under the edict of 1148 were given the choice between

---

[24] http://www.leaderu.com/ftissues/ft9511/opinion/opinion.html (4 June, 2010).

[25] http://genuinegopmom.blogspot.com/2010/03/is-america-experiencing-battered-wife.html (6 June, 2010).

[26] Philip Rhodes, *An Outline History of Medicine* (London: Butterworths, 1985), 25.

conversion to Islam, death or exile.[27] Maimonides wrote to the Jews in Yemen about the Islamic overlords: "the more we suffer and choose to conciliate them, the more they choose to act belligerently toward us."[28]

As the woman starts to accept the blame as the cause of the abusive relationship, she is despised by her male partner. A parallel scorn of the West and its history and values is sometimes shown by Muslims. The billionaire philanthropist and educationalist Fetullah Gulen, whose organization sponsors the Islamic chair in the Australian Catholic University in Melbourne, draws much of his inspiration from the teachings of Turkish philosopher Said Nursi (1873-1960). Nursi's contempt for Europe was open and plain. At a famous sermon in the Damascus mosque in 1911, he referred to "the Europeans' ignorance ... barbarity ... and bigotry in their religion." He claimed: "European civilization is not founded on virtue and guidance but rather on lust and passion, rivalry and oppression, and ... the present evils of civilization have prevailed over its virtues."[29]

There is sometimes an implied or stated sense of obligation in abusive relationships, as though the violent man is owed absolute obedience and total submission. He feels that he has a right to rule and to act in such an atrocious way. Samuel Huntingdon commented: "the underlying problem for the West is not Islamic fundamentalism. It is Islam, a different civilisation, whose people are convinced of the superiority of their culture and are obsessed with the inferiority of their power."[30] The superiority concept is first announced in the Qur'an to the Muslims: "You are the best of peoples evolved for mankind enjoining what is right forbidding what is wrong and believing in Allah." (Q.3:110)

---

[27] Ibn Warraq 'Introduction' in Andrew Bostom (ed.) *The Legacy of Jihad: Islamic Holy War and the Fate of Non-Muslims* (Amherst: Prometheus Books, 2005).

[28] Moses Maimonides *Epistle to the Jews of Yemen*, excerpts from Norman Stillman, *The Jews of Arab Lands: a History and Source Book* (Pennsylvania: The Jewish Publication Society of America, 1979), 241, 242.

[29] Bediuzzaman Said Nursi, *The Damascus Sermon* (Trans. Sukran Vahide, Malaysia: Solzer Publications, 1994), 19, 26.

[30] Huntington 1996, 217.

Allah's Apostle said, "I have been sent (as an Apostle) in the best of all the generations of Adam's offspring since their Creation" (Hadith al-Bukhari 4:757).

"The Prophet said, 'The best of you (people) are my generation, and the second best will be those who will follow them, and then those who will follow the second generation...Then will come some people who will make vows but will not fulfil them; and they will be dishonest and will not be trustworthy, and they will give their witness without being asked to give their witness, and fatness will appear among them."[31] Unfortunately the legacy of these statements is a wistful looking back to the time of Muhammad as 'the golden age' of Islam. Many Muslims often dismiss subsequent and more enlightened and tolerant periods of Islam as *bida* ("innovation"), a pejorative term describing faithless presumption and overt disobedience.

Having established in his own mind his superiority over the beaten woman and seeing her accept this state of affairs, the man begins to think of himself as invincible. Islam often exhibits a similar triumphalism. Nursi concludes: "*The future shall be Islam's and Islam's alone ... the divine determining and our fate is ... that ours is a brilliant future, while the European's is a dubious past... Europe and America are pregnant with Islam. One day they will give birth to an Islamic state.*" (italics his)[32] Many Muslims, looking at the changes that have occurred in the last century see Nursi's words as nothing less than prophetic. Some in Australia, such as Sydney's Fred Nile, have called for an unlikely moratorium on Muslim immigration, fearful of where this is all heading.

It is a similar fear about the future that causes an abused woman to put strategies in place to minimize further trauma. She is careful not to provoke her attacker, avoiding words and actions which might precipitate violence. Similarly many in the West are very circumspect about how they describe Islam, for fear of a violent backlash. The 74 page White Paper on Counter-Terrorism mentions 'Islam' and 'Muslim' on only two pages, despite admitting that

---

[31] Hadith al-Bukhari 8:686.

[32] Bediuzzaman Said Nursi *The Damascus Sermon* (Trans.Sukran Vahide, Malaysia: Solzer Publications, 1994), 14, 23.

"[t]he main source of international terrorism and the primary terrorist threat to Australia and Australian interests today comes from people who follow a distorted and militant interpretation of Islam that calls for violence as the answer to perceived grievances."[33]

How can we move forward? Some guidance may be found in counseling approaches to violent marriages. The steps to addressing pathological relationships, whether between couples or between communities, have some similarities.

The first step to resolution is a recognition that there is a problem. Living in denial about an abusive relationship is never healthy. While it is certainly true that most Muslims are not terrorists, it is equally true that most terrorists are Muslims. There is a problem here: Islam, intimidation and violence are connected.

Secondly the abused person must establish some inner convictions. The woman needs to recognise her own worth and stand up for her own rights. "I am valuable, important, and worthy of love and respect. I will not allow myself to be beaten, mistreated or abused." Australians, through hard work and good fortune, have been able to construct a nation that is peaceful and prosperous, free and fair. Moreover Australia has provided a safe and supportive haven for over a quarter of a million Muslims fleeing war, violence, corruption and poverty in their own countries. Australia should be proud of its achievements. Although Australia is not perfect, still there is much to be proud of as a nation.

Thirdly, an abusive man needs to recognise the intolerability of violence, and commit himself to peaceful and respectful means of understanding and addressing any differences. It is against the law to threaten or be violent towards another person.

Unfortunately some Muslims feel that violence against non-Muslims is sanctioned by their sacred texts (for example, the 'sword verses' of Q.9:5, 29) and also by the example of Muhammad who stated that ""I have been ordered (by Allah) to fight against the people until they testify that none has the right to be worshipped but Allah and that Muhammad is Allah's Apostle, ..." (Hadith

---

[33] http://www.dpmc.gov.au/publications/counter_terrorism/docs/counter-terrorism_white_paper.pdf (27 April, 2010), 8.

alBukhari 1:24). These concepts need to be recognised and acknowledged by the broader Muslim community, and addressed in ways that do not encourage aggression against others simply because they differ religiously.

Australia is held together by a series of widely-held values such as the rule of law, equality of all people, freedom of thought and expression, and the unacceptability of resolving differences by unlawful means. All Muslims in Australia must openly renounce violence, and seek to emulate these values. It is only then that all Australians, whether Muslim or not, will get a 'fair go.'

Using the Bible in Da'wa

Denis Savelyev

Introduction

Da'wa is an Arabic word, which has the primary meaning *call* or *invitation*. In the religious sense, the *da'wa* is the invitation, addressed to men by God and the prophets, to believe in the true religion, Islam.[1] Historically this term has acquired a number of meanings, but mainly it is understood as a religious outreach for the purpose of bringing deviant Muslims back to faith, or for the conversion of non-Muslims.[2] This appeal to conversion is made by missionary activity, rather than by force.[3] In this paper the term *da'wa* is used in the narrow sense of Muslim missionary activity aimed at the conversion of non-Muslims, and particularly Christians, to Islam.

There are numerous Muslim *da'wa* books, which talk about the Bible to varying degrees. In this paper we will examine four books, which have been written in different parts of the world during the last eighty years. In addition to their time-range and geographical criteria, these books were chosen due to their wide circulation and extensive use of the Biblical material.

The first book *Muhammad in the Bible*[4] is based on a series of articles written by a Christian convert to Islam, David Benjamin (d. c.1940), for *The Islamic Review* from June 1928 to August 1931. According to a controversial[5] biographical sketch, first published in the same magazine in February 1929, he was born in 1867 at Urmia

---

[1] M. Canard, "Da'wa" in *The Encyclopaedia of Islam*, ed. B. Lewis, Ch. Pellat and J. Schacht, (13 vols., Leiden, E.J.Brill, 1991, vol. 2), 168-170.

[2] "Daawa" in the *Encyclopedia of Islam*, ed. Juan E. Campo (New York, Facts on File, 2009), 177.

[3] "Da'wa" in the *Historical Dictionary of Islam*, ed. Ludwig W. Adamec (Lanham, The Scarecrow Press, 2009), 80.

[4] 'Abdu 'l-Ahad Dawud *Muhammad v Biblii*, per. 'Abd 'l-Ahad Madwar (Doha, Izdatelstvo Ministerstva Wakufov i Islamskih Otnosheniy, 1995).

[5] Mark Pleas, "David Benjamin Keldani – A bishop converts to Islam?" http://www.answering-islam.org/Hoaxes/keldani.html (1 November, 2010).

in Persia and in 1895 ordained as a Roman-Catholic priest. Later on he became disappointed in Christianity because of its "multitudinous shapes and colours" and "unauthentic, spurious and corrupted Scriptures".[6] He resigned and a few years later became a Muslim, taking on a new name 'Abdu 'l-Ahad Dawud'. *The Islamic Review* was founded in 1913 by the Ahmadiyya Movement, in order to "propagate Islam through newspapers in England".[7] Two series of articles by 'Abdu 'l-Ahad Dawud, "Muhammad in the Old Testament" and "Muhammad in the New Testament", published in *The Islamic Review*, were later compiled into a separate book, which was translated into at least four other languages: Arabic, Russian, German and Indonesian.

The next two books, or to be precise booklets, were written by Ahmed Hoosen Deedat (d. 2005). Born in 1918 in India, he migrated at a young age to South Africa, where he lived for the rest of his life. Deedat was the founder and president of the Islamic Propagation Centre International, the largest Islamic Dawah Organization in the world. He published more than 20 books and travelled all over the world, delivering lectures and engaging in public debates. His publications have been translated into many different languages: Russian, Urdu, Arabic, Bengali, French, Amharic, Chinese, Japanese, Indonesian, Zulu, Afrikaans, Dutch, and Norwegian, amongst others.[8] We will consider two of his booklets, *What the Bible Says About Muhammad pbuh*[9] and *Muhammad pbuh the Natural Successor to Christ*[10]. The former booklet talks about the Old Testament, the latter about the New Testament.

---

[6] "A Short Biographical Sketch of Professor 'Abdu 'l-Ahad Dawud, B.D.", *The Islamic Review*, XVII/2, (February, 1929), 76-78.

[7] "Founding of *The Islamic Review*, 1913" http://www.wokingmuslim.org/history/isrev/founding.htm (1 November, 2010).

[8] "IPCI – Welcome to Islam" http://www.ipci.co.za/frameset.asp (1 November, 2010).

[9] Ahmed Deedat, *What the Bible Says About Muhammad pbuh* (Durban, Islamic Propagation Centre International, 2005).

[10] Ahmed Deedat, *Muhammad pbuh the Natural Successor to Christ* (Durban, Islamic Propagation Centre International, 1997).

The last book *God's Judgment, Islam in the Bible – 200 prophecies!*[11] was written by Abdurahim Baymatov, a professor of Comparative Theology from Kyrgyzstan. This book is actively distributed in electronic form on Russian-speaking websites in Russia and in former Soviet Union countries. The author has no near-term plans to publish the book in hard copy in its current form in the Russian language; however it is going to be translated into Arabic and published in Egypt[12].

First we will examine the attitude of the above-mentioned authors towards the Bible. Then, we will look at the charges they level at the Bible, following which we will consider the alleged prophecies about Muhammad and Islam in the Bible. After that we will examine the methods of interpretation, or re-interpretation, of the Bible applied in these books, and their usage of extra-Biblical material.

Attitudes towards the Bible

From the beginning of Islam there have been a range of opinions concerning the integrity of the Bible. According to the foremost Hanbali jurist of the Middle Ages, Ibn Taymiyya[13] (d. 1328), there are three views on this issue, but in fact he cites four.[14] The first one is that there is no copy of the text that corresponds to what God revealed in the Torah and Gospel. One of the representatives of this point of view was the Andalusian jurist, historian, philosopher and theologian, Ibn Hazm (d.994). He attacked the Gospels, arguing that they show no guarantee of being a revealed text, and that they do not even achieve the credibility of hadith.[15] The second opinion is that the Bible was changed to a greater or lesser extent. An example of this viewpoint can be seen in the statements of Ka'b al-

---

[11] Abdurahim Baymatov, *Bozhiy Sud, Islam v Biblii – 200 prorochestv!* (2008). http://whyislam.ru/index/wp-content/uploads/2008/10/Boji_sud.pdf (1 November, 2010).

[12] From personal communication via e-mail with Abdurahim Baymatov.

[13] Oliver Leaman, "Ibn Taymiyya, Taqi Al-Din" in *The Qur'an – An Encyclopedia*, ed. Oliver Leaman (London, Routledge, 2006), 280.

[14] Abdulah Saeed *The Qur'an – an Introduction* (London, Routledge, 2008), 152.

[15] R. Arnaldez, "Ibn Hazm" in *The Encyclopaedia of Islam*, ed. B. Lewis, Ch. Pellat, and J. Schacht. (13 vols., Leiden, E. J. Brill, 1991, vol. 3), 790-796.

Ahbar (d. 652), a Yemenite Jew who converted to Islam shortly after the death of the Prophet Muhammad.[16] According to the Muslim tradition he specified ten Qur'anic verses which the Jews had allegedly erased from their scripture, because they contained predictions of the advent of Islam.[17] Another example of this opinion can be found in the works of an important jurisprudent, Qur'an commentator and historian, Muhammad b. Jarir al-Tabari (d. 923)[18]. In his *ta'rikh* he alludes to the textual corruption of the Bible by referring to the Jewish source as "the Torah, which is in their hands today" and to the Christian source as "the Torah that they (the Christians) possess".[19] The third point of view is that distortion was only in meaning, but not in the text. An example of this standpoint can be found in the commentaries of one of the greatest intellectuals in the history of Islam, the theologian and jurist al-Razi[20] (d. 1210). When explaining Qur'anic verses about *tahrif*, he, on one hand allowed the possibility of the text changing, and on the other, that the meaning had changed; but personally he leant towards the meaning having changed.[21] The fourth and last point of view, which according to Ibn Taymiyya was the correct one, is that there are different copies of the Bible, some of them distorted and some not. Thus:

> Whoever says that nothing in [these] copies [versions] was corrupted he has denied what cannot be denied. Whoever says that after the

---

[16] Rafik Berjak, "Isra'iliyyat" in *The Qur'an – An Encyclopedia*, ed. Oliver Leaman (London, Routledge, 2006), 323.

[17] John Wansbrough, *Quranic Studies* (New York, Prometheus Books, 2004), 189.

[18] Christopher Melchert "Tabari, Al- (839-923)", in the *Encyclopedia of Islam and the Muslim World*, ed. Richard C. Martin, (2 vols New York, Macmillan Reference USA, 2004, vol. 2), 671.

[19] Jane Dammen MacAuliffe, "The Prediction and Prefiguration of Muhammad" in the *Bible and Qur'an, Essays in Scriptural Integrity*, ed. John C. Reeves (Atlanta, Society of Biblical Literature, 2003), 121-122.

[20] A.H. Jones, "Al-Razi, Fakr al-Din", in *The Qur'an – An Encyclopedia*, ed. Oliver Leaman (London, Routledge, 2006), 530.

[21] Abdullah Saeed, "The Charge of Distortion of Jewish and Christian Scriptures", *Muslim World*, Vol. 92 Issue 3/4 (Fall 2002), 419-436.

Prophet [Muhammad] (peace be upon him) all copies [versions] have been distorted, he has said what is manifestly false[22]

Opinions in the modern world also differ. Two extremes are represented by the views of a Salafi scholar from Saudi Arabia, Muhammed Salih al-Munajjid, and Ulil Abshar-Abdalla, co-founder of the Liberal Islam Network of Indonesia. The former claims that the Qur'an abrogates all previous scriptures, which were distorted and altered, and that the only remaining authentic revealed scripture is the Qur'an.[23] The latter states that all scriptures are authentic and genuine.[24]

'Abdu 'l-Ahad Dawud, Ahmed Deedat and Abdurahim Baymatov take the middle view in this matter. They all use the Bible, implying that it has not been changed completely, and at the same time, they accuse Jews and Christians of changing the text and meaning of the Bible. Even so, their opinions on the extent of the corruption of the Bible vary significantly. According to Dawud almost the entire Bible has been corrupted. When talking about the New Testament Dawud states that there are only "a few scintillating sparkles" of truth left in the Gospels,[25] and that Christian beliefs are derived from the words that were put into the mouth of Jesus and of his Apostles, so despite the Qur'anic testimony that Jesus' apostles were holy men, their scriptures cannot be trusted, due to the later interpolations.[26] Baymatov is more careful in his statements about the distortion of the Bible. He quotes Qur'an 3:93 and 6:20 as proof that during his lifetime the Bible contained truth about Muhammad, otherwise Jews and Christians could not have known about Muhammad. He also quotes traditions from the Sira of Ibn Hisham and from Sahih Bukhari, which talk about the Jews and Christians who became Muslims, because they knew of the prophecies concerning Muhammad contained in the Bible.[27] Furthermore,

---

[22] Abdulah Saeed *The Qur'an – an Introduction*, 153.

[23] Abdulah Saeed *The Qur'an – an Introduction*, 153-154.

[24] Abdulah Saeed *The Qur'an – an Introduction*, 155.

[25] 'Abdu 'l-Ahad Dawud *Muhammad v Biblii*, 157.

[26] 'Abdu 'l-Ahad Dawud *Muhammad v Biblii*, 81.

[27] Abdurahim Baymatov, *Bozhiy Sud, Islam v Biblii – 200 prorochestv!*, 5-6.

Baymatov states that the prohibition on the translation of the Bible into English in 16th century England was made in order to hide the prophecies about Muhammad from lay people.[28] Deedat's opinion is closer to the views of Dawud. This can be seen from his claims that the Christian Scripture "abound in discrepancies", that there are 50 000 errors in the Bible[29], and that Christians have "24 000 manuscripts in their possession of which no two are identical".[30]

For all three authors the main criterion for differentiating the unchanged parts of the Bible from the distorted ones is their conformity to Islamic teachings. According to Dawud,

> It is absolutely impossible to get at the truth, the true religion, from these Gospels, unless they are read and examined from an Islamic and Unitarian point of view. It is only then that the truth can be extracted from the false, and the authentic distinguished from the spurious. It is the spirit and the faith of Islam, that can alone sift the Bible and cast away the chaff and error from its pages.[31]

Deedat claims that "the Qur'an had come to confirm, correct and complete Divine Revelation, or whatever was left of it in unworthy hands."[32] Baymatov states that "according to the instruction of Islam, everything in the Bible that conforms with the teaching of Islam can be used in disputes with the Christians, while we must keep pious silence about everything that does not conform to it".[33] The main difference between his approach to the Bible and those of Dawud and Deedat is that Baymatov prefers not to talk about the passages that conflict with Muslim beliefs, while Dawud and Deedat use these contradictions in order to attack the authenticity of the Bible. We will consider this method in more detail alongside the other methods of attacking the Bible in the next section of this paper.

---

[28] Abdurahim Baymatov, *Bozhiy Sud, Islam v Biblii – 200 prorochestv!*, 126.

[29] Ahmed Deedat, *What the Bible Says About Muhammad pbuh*, 21.

[30] Ahmed Deedat, *Muhammad pbuh the Natural Successor to Christ*, 25.

[31] 'Abdu 'l-Ahad Dawud *Muhammad v Biblii*, 148.

[32] Ahmed Deedat, *Muhammad pbuh the Natural Successor to Christ*, 19.

[33] Abdurahim Baymatov, *Bozhiy Sud, Islam v Biblii – 200 prorochestv!*, 6.

Attacking the Bible

One of the ways in which Muslims use the Bible in *da'wa* is to criticize it, in order to show its non-authenticity against the background of the Qur'an. The charges preferred against the Bible by Dawud, Deedat and Baymatov are several:

a) Absence of the Original Manuscripts of the Bible

Dawud makes a few self-contradictory comments regarding originals of the Bible. He states that the Gospel of Jesus never had a written form,[34] yet in another passage Dawud attacks Christianity because it "does not possess a single line in script from its supposed founder, Jesus Christ".[35] He also asks how it is possible that Jesus or his apostles did not leave a real and authentic Gospel, and why the Church has not preserved the original text of the real Gospel, or its translation,[36] and blames the Synod of Nicaea for the "irreparable loss of the Sacred Gospel in its original Aramaic text".[37] It is interesting that while stating that Jesus never authorized anybody to write the Gospel, Dawud repeatedly refers to the Gospel of Barnabas in order to support his point of view.[38]

b) Late Dates for the Appearance of the New Testament

Another method of criticizing the Bible used by Dawud is to claim that the Gospels were written only after the death of the eyewitnesses. He interprets the first verses of the Gospel of Luke as a statement that Luke wrote it a "long time after the death of all apostles".[39] He also argues that the complete New Testament became available for the Churches only after the Council of Nicaea.[40]

---

[34] 'Abdu 'l-Ahad Dawud *Muhammad v Biblii*, 59, 185.

[35] 'Abdu 'l-Ahad Dawud *Muhammad v Biblii*, 97.

[36] 'Abdu 'l-Ahad Dawud *Muhammad v Biblii*, 128.

[37] 'Abdu 'l-Ahad Dawud *Muhammad v Biblii*, 129.

[38] 'Abdu 'l-Ahad Dawud *Muhammad v Biblii*, 41, 81, 89-90, 98, 135, 139, 149, 158-159, 202.

[39] 'Abdu 'l-Ahad Dawud *Muhammad v Biblii*, 126.

[40] 'Abdu 'l-Ahad Dawud *Muhammad v Biblii*, 138-139.

c) Destruction of the True Scriptures

Dawud sites the following words of St. Ephraim, who wrote against the heresy of Bir Disin,

> Woe to unto thee o miserable Bir Disin
>
> That thou didst read the "word was God's"!
>
> But the Book [Gospel] did not write likewise
>
> Except that "the Word was God"

Dawud asserts that all the literature of the Unitarians was destroyed, save the quotations in the polemical writings of the Trinitarians, and based on the abovementioned citation from St. Ephraim makes a reverse statement, that the Trinitarians, since the beginning, have been accused of changing the Holy Book.[41]

Abdurahim Baymatov quotes from the book *The Apocalypses of Our Times* by Russian religious philosopher Vasiliy Rozanov (d.1919), who mentions the lost epistle of the Apostle Paul, arguing that it could not have been lost, but it must have been destroyed because of its blasphemous content;[42] and uses this statement to claim that the actual reason for the destruction of this letter was a clear message about Islam.[43]

d) Differences between Protestant and Catholic Canons of the Bible

Another charge leveled against the authenticity of the Bible is the difference between the two lists of books in Protestant and Catholic Bibles. This argument is used by Ahmed Deedat in the booklet *Muhammad pbuh the Natural Successor to Christ*.[44] Although he mentions this difference only in passing, he repeats the same argument in more detail in his other booklet *Is the Bible God's Word?*, to which he refers several times.[45] Based on the verses from the Book of Revelation 22:18-19,

---

[41] 'Abdu 'l-Ahad Dawud *Muhammad v Biblii*, 25-27.

[42] Abdurahim Baymatov, *Bozhiy Sud, Islam v Biblii – 200 prorochestv!*, 155.

[43] Abdurahim Baymatov, *Bozhiy Sud, Islam v Biblii – 200 prorochestv!*, 156.

[44] Ahmed Deedat, *Muhammad pbuh the Natural Successor to Christ*, 51.

[45] Ahmed Deedat, *Muhammad pbuh the Natural Successor to Christ*, 5, 25, 33, 51.

"...If anyone adds anything to them, God will add to him the plagues described in this book. And if anyone takes words away from this book of prophecy, God will take away from him his share in the tree of life an the holy city..."[46]

he underlines that Protestants "have bravely expunged seven whole books from their Book of God".[47]

e) Differences between the Translations of the Bible

Both Deedat and Baymatov refer to different translations of the Bible. Deedat cites the Book of Acts 2:16, "...this is what was spoken by the prophet Joel" and says that the name Joel was expunged from The New English Bible. Based on that he assumes that if Christians can edit out names of their prophets, they surely can do the same with the names like Ishmael and Ahmed.[48] Baymatov mentions differences between the Russian Synodal translation of the Bible and the translation made by the Jehovah's Witnesses. According to Baymatov the word Eagle in the Revelation 8:13 was changed to the Angel in order to hide a prophecy about Muhammad, since Baymatov believes that the Eagle is one of the symbols of Muhammad.[49]

f) Alteration and Interpolation of the Original Text of the Bible

Deedat and Dawud use the differences between Christian and Islamic beliefs to accuse Christians of changing the Word of God. Deedat discards the miracle of turning the water into wine (John 2:7-10), because according to Islam, alcohol is forbidden.[50] Both Deedat and Dawud state that Christians changed the original word *periklytos* – the praised one, or Ahmad, in John 14:16, 15:26 and 16:17.[51] Dawud uses this kind of argumentation quite often.

---

[46] Biblical quotations are taken from *The Holy Bible, New International Version* (Grand Rapids, Zondervan Publishing House, 1988).

[47] Ahmed Deedat, *Is the Bible God's Word?* (Durban, Islamic Propagation Centre International, 1992), 9.

[48] Ahmed Deedat, *Muhammad pbuh the Natural Successor to Christ*, 71.

[49] Abdurahim Baymatov, *Bozhiy Sud, Islam v Biblii – 200 prorochestv!*, 67.

[50] Ahmed Deedat, *Muhammad pbuh the Natural Successor to Christ*, 42.

[51] Ahmed Deedat, *Muhammad pbuh the Natural Successor to Christ*, 21. 'Abdu 'l-Ahad Dawud *Muhammad v Biblii*, 32.

According to him the original phrase in John 1:1 "...and the Word was God's", was changed to "...and the Word was God".[52] The name Ishmael in Genesis 22:2,6,7 was changed to Isaac[53], and the story of Esau's selling his birthright to Jacob was fabricated in order "to justify the ill-treatment ascribed to Ishmael".[54] The words of Jesus that John the Baptist was preparing the way for the coming king, Jesus, were fabricated "by some fanatical monk, or by an ignorant bishop",[55] since the coming king was Muhammad. John the Baptist could not say that Jesus was the Lamb of God, which takes away the sin of the word, because these words contradict Islamic monotheism and the teachings of John the Baptist in the Gospels.[56] The words of Jesus, "I go to my Father" in John 16:10, as well as the titles, "the Son of Josef", "the Son of David", "the Son of Man", "the Son of God", "the Son", "the Christ", and "the Lamb" were erroneously ascribed to Jesus.[57] Dawud states that the words of Jesus where he says that he will ask the Father to give another Comforter sound too arrogant to be truthful, and thus must have been changed. Based on his personal opinion he restores the verse, which according to him must have been as follows, "I shall go to the Father, and he shall send you another apostle, whose name shall be Periklytos, that he may remain with you for ever."[58] Dawud also argues that such verses as: "The Son of Man came to be served", "The Son of Man shall be delivered unto the hands of the Chief Priests and the Scribes", or "The Son of Man came eating and drinking [wine]" are late fabrications "written by Greek Christians, who did not know the Jewish Scriptures".[59]

---

[52] 'Abdu 'l-Ahad Dawud *Muhammad v Biblii*, 25.

[53] 'Abdu 'l-Ahad Dawud *Muhammad v Biblii*, 40.

[54] 'Abdu 'l-Ahad Dawud *Muhammad v Biblii*, 43.

[55] 'Abdu 'l-Ahad Dawud *Muhammad v Biblii*, 95, 96.

[56] 'Abdu 'l-Ahad Dawud *Muhammad v Biblii*, 152, 153.

[57] 'Abdu 'l-Ahad Dawud *Muhammad v Biblii*, 203, 206.

[58] 'Abdu 'l-Ahad Dawud *Muhammad v Biblii*, 196.

[59] 'Abdu 'l-Ahad Dawud *Muhammad v Biblii*, 216.

g) Mistakes

Although Deedat refers to the Jehovah's Witnesses journal to claim that there are 50 000 errors in the Bible[60], he mentions only one verse as containing a clear mistake. Ignoring the first chapter of Acts, where it is written that Matthias was added to the eleven apostles, Deedat states that the words in Acts 2:14 where "Peter stood up with the Eleven" could not be true because Judas at that time was dead.[61] Dawud also confuses the story about the shepherds in the second chapter of Luke with the story about the wise men and claims that there is a mistake, because the wise men could not have come from Persia so quickly.[62]

h) Contradictions

Deedat and Dawud cite a few passages in the Bible, which they consider as being contradictory. Deedat mentions the two genealogies of the Christ in the Gospels and refers his readers to his booklet, *Is the Bible God's word?* for a fuller explanation.[63] Dawud sees a contradiction in the narrations about the first meeting of Peter and Andrew with Jesus (John 1, Matthew 4:18-19, Mark 1:16-18). He also gives an example of contradictions in different passages talking about Jesus and John the Baptist.[64] It is important to add, that although there are not many examples of contradictions and mistakes given in the books examined in this paper, there are some Muslim books which are dedicated primarily to these topics. Mohamed Ghounem, for instance, in one of his books argues that the Qur'an corrects more than 200 errors in the Bible,[65] while Shabir Ally enumerates 101 contradictions in the Bible.[66]

---

[60] Ahmed Deedat, *What the Bible Says About Muhammad pbuh*, 21.

[61] Ahmed Deedat, *Muhammad pbuh the Natural Successor to Christ*, 70-71.

[62] 'Abdu 'l-Ahad Dawud *Muhammad v Biblii*, 124, 125.

[63] Ahmed Deedat, *Muhammad pbuh the Natural Successor to Christ*, 5.

[64] 'Abdu 'l-Ahad Dawud *Muhammad v Biblii*, 146.

[65] Mohamed Ghounem, *200+ Ways the Quran Corrects the Bible: How Islam Unites Judaism and Christianity* (USA, Multi-National Muslim Committee, 2004).

[66] Shabir Ally, *101 Clear Contradictions in the Bible* (Canada, Al-Attique Publishers Inc, no date).

i) Indecent Passages of the Bible

There are some verses in the Bible, which Muslims believe to be improper to be called the Word of God. Dawud and Deedat give several such passages, relating to the sins of the prophets. Dawud states that the Book of Genesis is full of falsehoods because in Genesis 22:10-20, 20:2-18 it is written that Abraham was a husband of his own sister, which according to the Moses' Law was punishable by death.[67] Likewise the story of Jacob, who was married to two sisters, could not also be true, as well as the story of Judah, who married his daughter in law, because according to Leviticus 18:18 and 20:12 it was a great sin.[68] The story of David and Bathsheba could not be true because David, as a prophet of God, must have been sinless.[69] Since, according to the Gospels, Jesus said that John the Baptist was Elias, while John said he was not, Deedat discredits this story, because in his opinion it implies that one of them was lying, which is impossible, because according to Islam both of them were great prophets.[70] Although Deedat mentions only one indecent passage in the two booklets examined in this paper, he dedicates another booklet almost entirely to this topic.[71]

Finding Prophecies about Muhammad and Islam in the Bible

The oldest method of using the Bible in da'wa is finding predictions about Muhammad and Islam in the Bible. This quest was inspired by several Qur'anic verses, such as Sura 7:157 "Those who follow the Messenger, the Prophet who can neither read nor write, whom they find written with them in the Taurat and the Injeel..."[72], Surah 2:129, where Abraham and Ishmael pray, "Our Lord! Send amongst them a Messenger of their own..." or Sura 61:6, where

---

[67] 'Abdu 'l-Ahad Dawud *Muhammad v Biblii*, 41.

[68] 'Abdu 'l-Ahad Dawud *Muhammad v Biblii*, 56.

[69] 'Abdu 'l-Ahad Dawud *Muhammad v Biblii*, 73-74.

[70] Ahmed Deedat, *What the Bible Says About Muhammad pbuh* 20-21.

[71] Ahmed Deedat, *Combat Kit* (Durban, Islamic Propagation Centre International, 1992).

[72] All Qur'anic quotations are taken from *The Noble Qur'an*, tr. Dr. Muhammad Taqi'-ud-Din AL-Hilali and Dr. Muhammad Muhsin Khan (Madinah, King Fahd Complex for the Printing of the Holy Qur'an, 1414 a.h.).

Jesus says that he came, "confirming the Taurat before me, and giving glad tidings of a Messenger to come after me, whose name shall be Ahmad". The first allusions to the Biblical verses talking about Muhammad can be found in the early biographies of Muhammad. According to Ibn Ishaq (d.770) Abu Talib said that Muhammad was a "prophet like Moses described in the oldest books".[73] Words, "prophet like Moses" is an allusion to Deuteronomy 18:18. Ibn Ishaq also narrates stories about two learned rabbis Abdullah b. Salam and Mukhayriq who became Muslims because they knew about Muhammad's name, description, and the time at which he appeared, and they were waiting for his coming.[74] Ibn Sa'd (d.845) in his historical dictionary, gives a paraphrase of Isaiah 35 and 42 as a description of Muhammad.[75] Some Biblical passages, invoked as prophecies about Muhammad, were cited in the debate (at the end of the 8th century) between the Nestorian Patriarch Timothy I and the Abbasid Caliph al-Mahdi. Al-Mahdi questioned Timothy I about passages in Deuteronomy, Isaiah and the Gospel of John.[76] The first formal list of predictions can be found in the letter of Ibn al-Layth, and the first extensive list of alleged prophecies about Muhammad was given by a Christian convert to Islam, Ibn Rabban in the middle of the 9th century.[77] Jewish and Christian converts to Islam, who had the text of the Bible, as well as ready-made collections of Messianic passages at their disposal,[78] made a significant contribution in the process of

---

[73] A. Guillaume (tr.), *The Life of Muhammad, a Translation of Ishaq's Sirat Rasul Allah* (Oxford, Oxford University Press, 1967), 232/160.

[74] A. Guillaume (tr.), *The Life of Muhammad, a Translation of Ishaq's Sirat Rasul Allah*, 353/240-354/242.

[75] Adang Camilla, *Muslim Writers on Judaism and The Hebrew Bible* (Leiden, E.J. Brill, 1996), 16-17.

[76] Clint Hackenburg, "An Arabic-to-English Translation of the Religious Debate Between the Nestorian Patriarch Timothy I and the Abbasid Caliph al-Mahdi" (The Ohio State University, Unpublished M.A. Thesis, 2009), 28-31.

[77] Adang Camilla, *Muslim Writers on Judaism and The Hebrew Bible*, 21, 110, 144.

[78] For example, in the Qumran Sectarian Literature of the first century BC, there is a list of Messianic prophecies, among which is a testimony about the prophet like Moses. See Devorah Dimant, "Qumran Sectarian Literature" in the *Jewish Writings of the Second Temple Period*, ed. Michael E. Stone (Philadelphia, Assen Fortress Press, 1984), 518.

recovering testimonies about Muhammad from the earlier revelations.[79]

Dawud, Deedat and Baymatov conjointly enumerate 150 testimonies about Muhammad and Islam from 25 different books of the Bible.[80] All these alleged prophecies can be divided into several, sometimes overlapping, categories: titles or names, symbols, descriptions, and events.

a) Names/Titles

The authors assert that the following names or titles belong to Muhammad: Shiloh, or Reconciler[81] (Genesis 49:10); Redeemer[82] (Job 19:25); Lord[83] (Psalm 110:1; Isaiah 40:1-4[84]); "Altogether lovely"[85], that is, Muhammad (Song of Solomon 5:16); Son of Man (Daniel 7;[86] Matthew 10:23[87]); "Desire of Nations"[88] or "Hemdah", that is, Muhammad (Haggai 2:7-9); Messiah[89] (Matthew 22:41-46); "Eudokia" or "Good will" in the original language was Ahmadie, that is, Muhammad[90] (Luke 2:14); "Parakletos", which according to the authors must have been "Periklytos", or "Praised One", or

---

[79] Adang Camilla, *Muslim Writers on Judaism and The Hebrew Bible*, 142.

[80] See Appendix for a detailed comparative table.

[81] 'Abdu 'l-Ahad Dawud *Muhammad v Biblii*, 57-62; Abdurahim Baymatov, *Bozhiy Sud, Islam v Biblii – 200 prorochestv!*, 166.

[82] 'Abdu 'l-Ahad Dawud *Muhammad v Biblii*, 90.

[83] 'Abdu 'l-Ahad Dawud *Muhammad v Biblii*, 87-92; Abdurahim Baymatov, *Bozhiy Sud, Islam v Biblii – 200 prorochestv!*, 38.

[84] 'Abdu 'l-Ahad Dawud *Muhammad v Biblii*, 163.

[85] Ahmed Deedat, *What the Bible Says About Muhammad pbuh*, 5.

[86] 'Abdu 'l-Ahad Dawud *Muhammad v Biblii*, 63-71, 216-236.

[87] Abdurahim Baymatov, *Bozhiy Sud, Islam v Biblii – 200 prorochestv!*, 15.

[88] 'Abdu 'l-Ahad Dawud *Muhammad v Biblii*, 31; Abdurahim Baymatov, *Bozhiy Sud, Islam v Biblii – 200 prorochestv!*, 150.

[89] 'Abdu 'l-Ahad Dawud *Muhammad v Biblii*, 59.

[90] 'Abdu 'l-Ahad Dawud *Muhammad v Biblii*, 125-134, 140-144.

"Ahmad", that is, Muhammad[91] (John 14:16-26, 15:26, 16:7-13); "That prophet" in John 1:25 is a prophet like Moses – Muhammad;[92] also Muhammad is King of Kings and Lord of Lords[93] (Revelation 19:11-21). In most of these cases the authors try to find words which have the same Arabic root HMD, in order to prove that these prophecies are about Muhammad.

b) Symbols

Baymatov finds in the Bible various symbols, which, in his opinion, designate Muhammad and different aspects of Islam.[94] The symbol of Muhammad is the "Eagle from the East",[95] so he is prefigured in the following verses: Exodus 19:4-6; Deuteronomy 32:10-11; Isaiah 40:1-4, 41:25-27, 46:11-13, 48:14-15; Hosea 8:1,2; Revelation 4:7, 8:13. The phrase "New Song" is a symbol of the Qur'an[96], since the Qur'an is chanted. Thus, when David urges in the Psalms to sing a new song (Psalms 33:3, 96:1, 98:1, 144:9, 149:1)[97] – he is prophesying about the revelation of the Qur'an. When Isaiah mentions a new song and Kedar in the same passage (Isaiah 42:9-17), it is even more precise prophecy, since Baymatov believes that Muhammad is a descendant of Kedar.[98] The people in white robes in Revelation, who sing a new song (Revelation 5:9, 14:1-3, 15:2-3) – chant the Qur'an, which demonstrates that Islam is the true religion.[99] The "New/Everlasting/Better Covenant", according to

---

[91] 'Abdu 'l-Ahad Dawud *Muhammad v Biblii*, 139, 192, 202-203; Ahmed Deedat, *Muhammad pbuh the Natural Successor to Christ*, 15, 21, 26-27, 39; Abdurahim Baymatov, *Bozhiy Sud, Islam v Biblii – 200 prorochestv!*, 89, 92-93.

[92] 'Abdu 'l-Ahad Dawud *Muhammad v Biblii*, 147-148; Ahmed Deedat, *What the Bible Says About Muhammad pbuh*, 20-21; Abdurahim Baymatov, *Bozhiy Sud, Islam v Biblii – 200 prorochestv!*, 15.

[93] Abdurahim Baymatov, *Bozhiy Sud, Islam v Biblii – 200 prorochestv!*, 38.

[94] We will consider the more detailed explanation of the symbols used by Baymatov in the paragraph regarding re-interpretation of the Bible in the light of Islamic teaching.

[95] Abdurahim Baymatov, *Bozhiy Sud, Islam v Biblii – 200 prorochestv!*, 12, 30, 59, 60, 61, 66, 67.

[96] Abdurahim Baymatov, *Bozhiy Sud, Islam v Biblii – 200 prorochestv!*, 58-59.

[97] Abdurahim Baymatov, *Bozhiy Sud, Islam v Biblii – 200 prorochestv!*, 7, 11.

[98] Abdurahim Baymatov, *Bozhiy Sud, Islam v Biblii – 200 prorochestv!*, 7-8, 14, 16-19, 100, 132.

[99] Abdurahim Baymatov, *Bozhiy Sud, Islam v Biblii – 200 prorochestv!*, 7-8, 14, 154.

Baymatov, signifies the new and the last religion of Islam (Jeremiah 31:31, 32:40, 33:14-18; Ezekiel 37:26; Hebrews 7:22, 8:6, 12:25-29).[100] Some times Baymatov uses terms "New Song" and "New Covenant" interchangeably. The Sun is seen as a symbol of the true religion of God - Islam[101] (Isaiah 19:18, 21:11,12, 30:26, 60:1-3; Habakkuk 3:3-4, 11-13; Zechariah 14:6-7; Matthew 13:43; Revelation 1:16, 7:1-3, 10:1-7, 12:1-2, 16:8-9, 12, 19:17-18).[102]

c) Descriptions

Deedat, Baymatov and Dawud find descriptions of Muhammad in the following passages: According to Deedat Deuteronomy 18:18-19, which speaks about the prophet like Moses, depicts Muhammad, who came from the Arabs (the brothers of the Jews), and spoke only what he heard from Allah.[103] In the view of Baymatov, Muhammad is described in the Bible as a great and beautiful king, husband, father and warrior (Psalm 45:1-18);[104] a person who received a scroll, despite the fact that he could not read (Isaiah 29:12);[105] as a righteous man from the east, who is coming from Edom and Bozrah with red garments, and to whom God handed over the nations, and subdued the kings to him (Isaiah 41:1-3; 63:7);[106] and as the one who brings good tidings (Isaiah 41:25-27, 52:7; Nahum 1:15), since in Surah 48:8 Muhammad is called a bearer of glad tidings.[107] According to Dawud, Muhammad is described as the Son of Man who establishes judgment and unifies kingdom and religion (Daniel 7),[108] and as the one who will come after John the Baptist to baptize with the Holy Spirit and with fire,

---

[100] Abdurahim Baymatov, *Bozhiy Sud, Islam v Biblii – 200 prorochestv!*, 8-9.

[101] Abdurahim Baymatov, *Bozhiy Sud, Islam v Biblii – 200 prorochestv!*, 58-59.

[102] Abdurahim Baymatov, *Bozhiy Sud, Islam v Biblii – 200 prorochestv!*, 31, 43, 46, 48-49, 52-54 57, 60, 130, 134.

[103] Ahmed Deedat, *What the Bible Says About Muhammad pbuh*, 5-22.

[104] Abdurahim Baymatov, *Bozhiy Sud, Islam v Biblii – 200 prorochestv!*, 89-92.

[105] Ahmed Deedat, *What the Bible Says About Muhammad pbuh*, 12.

[106] Abdurahim Baymatov, *Bozhiy Sud, Islam v Biblii – 200 prorochestv!*, 2, 117.

[107] Abdurahim Baymatov, *Bozhiy Sud, Islam v Biblii – 200 prorochestv!*, 48-49, 147-149.

[108] 'Abdu 'l-Ahad Dawud *Muhammad v Biblii*, 63-82, 113-114, 216-236.

and to separate wheat from the chaff (Matthew 3:11-12; Luke 3:16-17).[109] In Dawud's viewpoint Jesus describes Muhammad as the least one, meaning the youngest one, in the kingdom of heaven, who is greater than John the Baptist (Matthew 11:11; Luke 7:28), and who was before him (John 1:15) because according to the Gospel of Barnabas, Muhammad's spirit preexisted before John the Baptist.[110]

d) Events

The last group of prophecies about Islam in the Bible are predictions of particular events related to the appearance of Islam, events happening in current times, and the events of the last days.

Dawud and Baymatov perceive Muhammad as a blessing for all nations, promised to Abraham.[111] Arabia is believed to be the land of "the shadow of death" that will see a great light (Isaiah 9:12; 21:11-12),[112] and Arabs are the ones taking the kingdom from the Jews (Isaiah 65:15; Matthew 21:43),[113] establishing the eternal kingdom of Islam and defeating the polytheistic Christians (Daniel 2, 8; Isaiah 41:1-3, 45:1-3; 46:11-13).[114] Baymatov believes that the Bible speaks about such events as the escape of the first Muslims to Ethiopia (Revelation 12:6-7),[115] Muhammad's escape from Makkah to Medina (Isaiah 21:13-15), and the Muslim victory in the battle of Badr (Islaiah 21:16-17).[116]

There are several passages in the Bible that Baymatov interprets as speaking of events of current times, related to Islam and Muslims.

---

[109] 'Abdu 'l-Ahad Dawud *Muhammad v Biblii*, 145-163, 175-184.

[110] 'Abdu 'l-Ahad Dawud *Muhammad v Biblii*, 139, 158-159.

[111] 'Abdu 'l-Ahad Dawud *Muhammad v Biblii*, 38-39; Abdurahim Baymatov, *Bozhiy Sud, Islam v Biblii – 200 prorochestv!*, 13.

[112] Abdurahim Baymatov, *Bozhiy Sud, Islam v Biblii – 200 prorochestv!*, 46, 57.

[113] Ahmed Deedat, *Muhammad pbuh the Natural Successor to Christ*, 11; Abdurahim Baymatov, *Bozhiy Sud, Islam v Biblii – 200 prorochestv!*, 2, 30, 61, 117.

[114] 'Abdu 'l-Ahad Dawud *Muhammad v Biblii*, 30, 163; Abdurahim Baymatov, *Bozhiy Sud, Islam v Biblii – 200 prorochestv!*, 103.

[115] Abdurahim Baymatov, *Bozhiy Sud, Islam v Biblii – 200 prorochestv!*, 22.

[116] Abdurahim Baymatov, *Bozhiy Sud, Islam v Biblii – 200 prorochestv!*, 21-22, 57.

He argues that the appearance of the modern state of Israel is foretold in Isaiah 11:12, 14:2 and is contrary to God's will, who according to His promise in Genesis 49:10, has already transferred the scepter of Judah to Muhammad.[117] Referring to Isaiah 14:3-15, Baymatov notes that Lucifer wanted to establish his throne in the sides of the North, and since all Northern Countries in our days are Christian, it means that they are under the power of Satan. The promise of God to break the staff of the wicked and to destroy pagan rulers relates to Christian countries, which are ruling the world.[118] Furthermore, Baymatov argues that the beast with ten horns in Revelation 13 is the European Union, which persecutes Muslims.[119]

Based on the system of signs, which will be discussed in the next part of this paper, Baymatov believes that Biblical prophecies about the last days speak about the final struggle and victory of Islam.[120] According to Baymatov the Bible predicts that Christians will continue to persecute Muslims and finally will start a war against them all over the Middle East; and the Second Coming of Christ, who will come to help Muslims, will then put Christian dominance to an end, and Muslims will inherit the earth forever.[121]

Interpretation of the Bible in the Light of Islamic Teachings

Although the previous section of this paper discussed the re-interpretation of the Bible, it was dedicated exclusively to alleged prophecies about Islam in the Bible. In this section we will examine the other methods of re-interpretation of the Bible used by Deedat, Dawud, and Baymatov. Generally, they are trying to shift the focus of the Bible from the redemptive sacrifice of Jesus Christ to

---

[117] Abdurahim Baymatov, *Bozhiy Sud, Islam v Biblii – 200 prorochestv!*, 99, 166-167.

[118] Abdurahim Baymatov, *Bozhiy Sud, Islam v Biblii – 200 prorochestv!*, 70, 117, 146.

[119] Abdurahim Baymatov, *Bozhiy Sud, Islam v Biblii – 200 prorochestv!*, 68-70, 132.

[120] See Appendix for the list of Biblical passages invoked by Baymatov as prophecies about the last days.

[121] Abdurahim Baymatov, *Bozhiy Sud, Islam v Biblii – 200 prorochestv!*, 12, 30-32, 37, 43-45, 48-49, 53, 57, 60, 66-67, 69, 94-98, 117, 129-136, 141, 143-146, 151-153.

monotheism and keeping the law. They try to demonstrate that Jesus was just a prophet, and that he came to fulfill the law.

Deedat, for example, says that Jesus was only a prophet for the Jews, that he never converted a single Gentile.[122] Baymatov gives the following list of Biblical verses in order to show the human nature of Christ:[123] John 14:28 "The father is greater than I"; Matthew 20:23 "to sit at my right or left is not for me to grant. These places belong to those for whom they have been prepared by my Father"; Matthew 12:32 "anyone who speaks a word against the Son of Man will be forgiven, but anyone who speaks against the Holy Spirit will not be forgiven"; Matthew 19:17 "Why do you ask me about what is good?"... "There is only One who is good"; Mark 13:32 "no one knows about that day or hour, not even the angels in heaven, nor the Son, but only the Father". Baymatov also discards the need for a redemptive sacrifice by referring to Isaiah 1:11-18 and asking the rhetorical question – if God did not want the blood of bulls, lambs and goats, why does he need the blood of a Messiah?[124]

All three authors use Matthew 5:17-18[125] to demonstrate that Jesus did not bring a new law, but came only to fulfill the law. Baymatov states that the words that Jesus is a mediator of a New Testament (Hebrew 7:22, 8:6, 9:15 and 12:24) mean that Jesus did not receive it, but he was only interceding for it.[126] Apart from re-interpreting individual verses of the Bible, Baymatov in his book tries to re-interpret the whole Bible based on the system of signs, which we will consider below.

Baymatov gives several sets of symbols. The main symbols are as follows:[127] the Sun is a symbol of God (Psalm 84:11); a star is a symbol of Christ (Revelation 22:16; Matthew 2:2); the sky is a

---

[122] Ahmed Deedat, *Muhammad pbuh the Natural Successor to Christ*, 17-18.

[123] Abdurahim Baymatov, *Bozhiy Sud, Islam v Biblii – 200 prorochestv!*, 153.

[124] Abdurahim Baymatov, *Bozhiy Sud, Islam v Biblii – 200 prorochestv!*, 158-159.

[125] Ahmed Deedat, *Muhammad pbuh the Natural Successor to Christ*, 18; Ahmed Deedat, *What the Bible Says About Muhammad pbuh*, 11; Abdurahim Baymatov, *Bozhiy Sud, Islam v Biblii – 200 prorochestv!*, 132; 'Abdu 'l-Ahad Dawud *Muhammad v Biblii*, 59.

[126] Abdurahim Baymatov, *Bozhiy Sud, Islam v Biblii – 200 prorochestv!*, 9, 158-159.

[127] Abdurahim Baymatov, *Bozhiy Sud, Islam v Biblii – 200 prorochestv!*, 58-59.

symbol of God's glory (Psalm 19:1); the Moon is a symbol of persecuted true religion (Joel 2:31); the stars are a symbol of the holy and chosen people of the last days (Daniel 12:3); the woman clothed in the sun is the religion of truth in the last days; an eagle is a symbol of holy people, the kingdom of priests; a new song is a symbol of God's last teaching (Psalm 96:1-3); the bear is a symbol of the Media-Persian Empire and the empire of the Antichrist in the last days (Revelation 13:1-3).

Baymatov's second set of symbols is a set of symbols from the Book of Revelation (21:1-2; 4:6-7; 5:6): The New Heaven is a declaration of the New Word of God (Psalm 19:1); a New Earth is a New Humanity (Psalm 33:3-8); No Sea means no pagans (Isaiah 57:20); a Woman prepared as a bride is the religion of truth in the last days (Revelation 12:14; Isaiah 46:11-13, 19:18-25); the Lion is a symbol of courage in the way of God (Proverbs 28:1); the Calf is a symbol of strength and energy (Proverbs 14:4); the Animal with a human face is humanity; the Eagle is Muhammad; the Lamb as if it had been slain is Jesus who was not really slain, but who Christians thought was slain.

The last set of symbols Baymatov uses is a set of signs of the holy chosen people of the last days.[128] This holy people will: Swear by the name of God (Isaiah 65:13-16); Sing a New Song – the Qur'an (Psalm 96:1-3; Isaiah 42:9-16); will be circumcised in heart and flesh (Ezekiel 44:9); will make blood sacrifices (Ezekiel 42-44; Isaiah 60:7; Revelation 9:13-15); will forbid pork and alcohol (Isaiah 66:16-17); will forbid idol worshiping (Isaiah 45:20); will forbid usury (1 Corinthians 6:9-10); will be persecuted by pagans (Isaiah 14:5-6; Revelation 13:7; Daniel 12:7; Revelation 14:1-7); and will be a kingdom of priests in Arabia (Habakkuk 3:3-10; Daniel 11:14-45).

In most cases the symbols are supported by only one Biblical verse, and sometimes are used interchangeably. For example, an Eagle signifies both Muhammad and a holy people. The holy people are a kingdom of priests, which also are symbolized by stars. A New Song signifies both the Qur'an and New Teaching. Some symbols have no Biblical support at all, for example, Baymatov states that an animal with the human face in Revelation signifies humanity, but gives no Biblical verse and does not explain what it means.

---

[128] Abdurahim Baymatov, *Bozhiy Sud, Islam v Biblii – 200 prorochestv!*, 38-40.

Although Baymatov claims that his book contains the greatest systematic miracle of Islam in the Bible,[129] close examination shows that this system is based on a random selection of verses.

Usage of Extra-Biblical Texts

Apart from using the Bible, Dawud, Deedat and Baymatov refer, to varying degrees, to some extra-Biblical materials.

As was mentioned in the second section of this paper, Ahmed Deedat refers to the Deuterocanonical books of the Catholic Bible in order to accuse Protestants of expunging God's Word from the Bible.[130]

Baymatov refers to the translation made by the Jehovah's Witnesses. He notices the difference in translation of Revelation 8:13. The Russian Synodal translation of the Bible uses the word "angel" in this verse, while in the Jehovah's Witnesses translation the word "eagle" is used. Baymatov uses this difference in order to show that Christians changed some verses of the Bible to hide prophecies about Muhammad.[131] Baymatov also mentions the lost epistle of Apostle Paul. Based on his own interpretation of Paul's teachings in the Bible in the light of Islam, Baymatov alleges that this epistle was destroyed by Christians because it contained clear Islamic teachings.[132]

Dawud repeatedly refers to the Gospel of Barnabas, which obviously influenced his own point of view. He says that according to the Gospel of Barnabas God made his covenant with Ishmael and that the most honorable man was from his line and not from the line of Isaac and David.[133] Dawud discards Paul's letters, because according to the Gospel of Barnabas Paul erred and led Christians to erroneous beliefs.[134] Based on the statements in the Gospel of Barnabas Dawud argues that Jesus was preparing the

---

[129] Abdurahim Baymatov, *Bozhiy Sud, Islam v Biblii – 200 prorochestv!*, 2.

[130] Ahmed Deedat, *Muhammad pbuh the Natural Successor to Christ*, 51.

[131] Abdurahim Baymatov, *Bozhiy Sud, Islam v Biblii – 200 prorochestv!*, 67.

[132] Abdurahim Baymatov, *Bozhiy Sud, Islam v Biblii – 200 prorochestv!*, 155-160.

[133] 'Abdu 'l-Ahad Dawud *Muhammad v Biblii*, 41, 89-90.

[134] 'Abdu 'l-Ahad Dawud *Muhammad v Biblii*, 81.

way for Muhammad, and not John the Baptist for Jesus.[135] While interpreting the angelic hymn in Luke 2:14, Dawud observes that the Gospel of Barnabas does not mention the hymn, nor the story of shepherds.[136] Dawud adopts the idea of the preexistence of the spirit of Muhammad in paradise. He mentions several times, that according to the Gospel of Barnabas Jesus spoke a lot about the glory of the spirit of Muhammad, that the spirit of Muhammad was created before any other thing, and because of that Jesus found himself unworthy to untie the lace on Muhammad's shoes.[137] Dawud makes the statement that Jesus said that the Messiah is not a Jew, and not the son of David, but the son of Ishmael, whose name will be Ahmad, who will establish God's kingdom by God's word, and by the sword.[138] Dawud does not acknowledge any source of these words, but it is most likely that he based them on the Gospel of Barnabas, since according to this Gospel Jesus repeatedly says that the Messiah is Muhammad, who will be from the line of Ishmael, and who will come with power upon the ungodly and destroy the idols and idolaters.[139]

In addition to the Gospel of Barnabas, Dawud uses the Apocalypse of Enoch. He uses only the compendium of the Book in an Encyclopedia because "Jewish Apocalypses" are inaccessible to him,[140] and notices in advance that Apocalypses were interpolated by Christians. Dawud gives the following summary:

> The Apocalypse of Enoch foretells the appearance of the Son of Man at a moment when the small flock of the sheep, though vigorously defended by a ram, will be fiercely attacked by the birds of prey from above and by the carnivorous beast on land. Among the enemies of the little flock are seen many other goats and sheep that had gone astray. The lord of the flock, like a good shepherd, suddenly appears and strikes the earth with his rod or scepter; it opens its mouth and

---

[135] 'Abdu 'l-Ahad Dawud *Muhammad v Biblii*, 98.

[136] 'Abdu 'l-Ahad Dawud *Muhammad v Biblii*, 135.

[137] 'Abdu 'l-Ahad Dawud *Muhammad v Biblii*, 139, 149, 158-159, 202.

[138] 'Abdu 'l-Ahad Dawud *Muhammad v Biblii*, 119.

[139] *The Gospel of Barnabas*, ed. Lonsdale and Laura Ragg (Karachi: Asaf Publications, 1982), 54-57, 103-104, 121-122.

[140] 'Abdu 'l-Ahad Dawud *Muhammad v Biblii*, 233.

swallows up the assailing enemy; chases and drives away from the pastures the rest of the pernicious birds and brutes. Then a sword is given to the flock as an emblem of power and the weapon of destruction. After which the flock is no longer headed by a ram but by a white bull with two large black horns.[141]

Dawud then interprets this vision from an Islamic point of view. The flock signifies true believers among Christians and Jews. A ram defending the flock is Arius, or some spiritual Unitarian leader who was defending true Christianity from Trinitarian doctrines. The Son of Man, who saves the flock is Muhammad who overcomes the pagan rulers, and the white bull is a symbol of Imam – an Islamic spiritual leader.[142] In conclusion Dawud mentions other Apocalypses, which bear the names of Moses, Baruch, Ezra, the Jubilees, and the Oracula Sibylliana, and states that if they would be studied impartially they would prove to be fulfilled in Muhammad and Islam.[143] The main reason why Dawud refers to these Apocalypses is to show the victorious character of the Son of Man in order to demonstrate that verses in the Bible which talk about the suffering of the Son of Man are just later fabrications, and that the real Son of Man was not Jesus, but Muhammad.

Conclusion

Although the main topic of the books examined in this paper concern the prediction of Muhammad in the Bible, the authors engage in different methods of using the Bible in their *da'wa*. On one hand, all the authors believe that the Bible was changed, and in order to prove this they level different charges against the Bible, such as: an absence of the original manuscripts, the late dates of the appearance of the New Testament, the destruction of the original Scriptures, the differences between the Catholic and Protestant canons of the Bible, the differences between the different translations of the Bible, alterations and interpolations of the Bible, mistakes in the Bible, contradictions in the Bible, and the presence of indecent passages in the Bible. On the other hand all the authors believe that there are at least some unchanged parts in the Bible,

---

[141] 'Abdu 'l-Ahad Dawud *Muhammad v Biblii*, 233.

[142] 'Abdu 'l-Ahad Dawud *Muhammad v Biblii*, 233-236.

[143] 'Abdu 'l-Ahad Dawud *Muhammad v Biblii*, 237.

which can be identified if someone examines them from the Islamic point of view. In practice this means that everything that speaks about the unity of God, keeping the law, the human nature of Christ, or anything that can be used as a prediction about Muhammad was not changed. Alternatively, everything that contradicts Islamic teachings is deemed to be a distortion or interpolation in the Bible. Decisions rest entirely on the authors' opinions without the use of any manuscript evidence. The same is true regarding the use of extra-Biblical materials. Anything in non-canonical literature that can be used to prove the Islamic point of view is deemed authentic by virtue. Dawud, Deedat and Baymatov use the "unchanged" parts of the Bible in two ways: by invoking different passages as prophecies about Muhammad and Islam, and by re-interpreting the Bible in the light of Islamic beliefs, that is by attempting to demonstrate that the main focus of the Bible is adherence to strict monotheism and keeping the law.

Appendix

Biblical Passages Invoked as Testimonies to Muhammad and Islam[144]

	Bible	Abd al-Ahad Dawood		Ahmeed Hoosen Deedat		Abdurahim Baymatov	
1	Gen. 15:4	38-39	Ishmael				
2	Gen. 16:12,15			W13[145]	Ishmael		
3	Gen. 17:23,25			W13	Ishmael		
4	Gen. 25:18			W13	Ishmael		
5	Gen. 49:10	57-62	Muhammad			166	Muhammad
6	Exod. 19:4-6					60	Islam
7	Deut. 18:18			W5	Muhammad		
8	Deut. 18:19			W18	Muhammad		
9	Deut. 32:10-11					59	Muhammad

---

[144] The figures in the table refer to page numbers.

[145] *What the Bible Says About Muhammad pbuh*

	Bible	Abd al-Ahad Dawood	Ahmeed Hoosen Deedat	Abdurahim Baymatov	
10	Deut. 33:2		M56[146] Muhammad	84	Muhammad
11	2 Chron. 7:13-14			32	Muslims
12	Job 19:25	90 Muhammad			
13	Psalm 33:3			7,10	Qur'an
14	Psalm 37:22,29			130	Muslims/LD[147]
15	Psalm 45:1-18			89	Muhammad
16	Psalm 96:1			7,11	Qur'an
17	Psalm 98:1			7,11	Qur'an
18	Psalm 110:1	87-92 Muhammad			
19	Psalm 144:9			7,11	Qur'an
20	Psalm 149:1			7,11	Qur'an
21	S.of S. 5:16		W5 Muhammad		
22	Isaiah 8:7			135	LD/Muslims
23	Isaiah 9:1-2			46	Islam
24	Isaiah 11:12			99,167	CT[148]/Israel
25	Isaiah 14:2			99,167	CT/Israel
26	Isaiah 14:3-5			146	LD
27	Isaiah 14:5,6			70, 117	LD
28	Isaiah 14:12-15			70	CT/LD
29	Isaiah 19:18			43	Islam/Muslims
30	Isaiah 19:19-25			44,45	Islam/Muslims
31	Isaiah 21:1-17			21-22,57	Islam

---

[146] *Muhammad pbuh the Natural Successor to Christ*

[147] Last Days – events related to the second coming of Jesus Christ and God's punishment of this world.

[148] Current Times – events related to the situation and events in current times

	Bible	Abd al-Ahad Dawood	Ahmeed Hoosen Deedat	Abdurahim Baymatov	
32	Isaiah 29:12		W17 Muhammad		
33	Isaiah 30:26			57	Muslims
34	Isaiah 34:2-6			117	LD
35	Isaiah 40:1-4	163 Muhammad			
36	Isaiah 41:1-3			2,61	Muhammad
37	Isaiah 41:25-27			61,149	Muhammad
38	Isaiah 42:10			7	Qur'an
39	Isaiah 42:9-17			132	LD/Qur'an
40	Isaiah 42:9-16			8,16-19,100	Qur'an
41	Isaiah 43:6-8			34	Muslims
42	Isaiah 45:1-3	163 Muhammad		32	LD/Muslims
43	Isaiah 46:11-13			2,30	Muhammad
44	Isaiah 48:14-15			61	Muhammad
45	Isaiah 52:1			129	LD/Muslims
46	Isaiah 52:7			147	Muhammad
47	Isaiah 56:7			133	LD/Muslims
48	Isaiah 60:1-3			31,43,60	LD/Muslims
49	Isaiah 60:6-7			30,131	LD/Muslims
50	Isaiah 63:1-6			117	LD/Muslims
51	Isaiah 65:15			117	Muslims/LD
52	Isaiah 66:15-17			31	LD/Muslims
53	Jeremiah 28:9	104, 105 Islam			
54	Jeremiah 31:31			8	Qur'an
55	Jeremiah 32:40			8	Qur'an/Islam
56	Jeremiah 33:14-18			8	Islam
57	Ezekiel 37:26			9	Islam

	Bible	Abd al-Ahad Dawood		Ahmeed Hoosen Deedat		Abdurahim Baymatov	
58	Ezekiel 40:38,39, 41-43,47					130,131	LD/Muslims
59	Ezekiel 41-46					136	LD/Muslims
60	Ezekiel 42:13					133	LD/Muslims
61	Ezekiel 43:1-5					130	LD/Muslims
62	Ezekiel 43:27					132	LD/Muslims
63	Ezekiel 44:9					32	LD/Muslims
64	Ezekiel 44:29					132	LD/Muslims
65	Ezekiel 46:20,24					132	LD/Muslims
66	Daniel 2:44					103	Islam
67	Daniel 7	63-71, 72-82, 113-114, 216-236	Muhammad/Islam				
68	Daniel 8	30	Islam/Muhammad				
69	Daniel 9:27					133,141	LD/Muslims
70	Daniel 10-12					94-98	LD/Muslims
71	Hosea 8:1,2					12,66	Islam/Muslims
72	Micah 1:2-5					117	LD
73	Micah 5:10,11					117	LD
74	Nahum 1:15					148	Muhammad
75	Habak. 3:3,4					46,84,99	Muhammad/Ka'ba/Islam
76	Habak. 3:3-13					48,49, 79-84	Islam
77	Zeph. 3:8-13					146	LD
78	Haggai 2:7-9	31	Muhammad			150	Muhammad/Islam
79	Haggai 2:22					146	LD
80	Zech. 6:13					131	LD/Muslims

	Bible	Abd al-Ahad Dawood		Ahmeed Hoosen Deedat		Abdurahim Baymatov	
81	Zech. 12:2,3					67,143	LD/Muslims
82	Zech. 12:4,5					144	LD/Muslims
83	Zech. 12:5,6					145	LD/Islam
84	Zech. 12:8,9					143	LD
85	Zech. 13:2,3					178	LD/Islam
86	Zech. 13:8					146	LD/Muslims
87	Zech. 14:1-5					143	LD/Muslims
88	Zech. 14:6,7					43	Islam
89	Zech. 14:14					67,143	LD/Muslims
90	Zech. 14:20,21					117,133	LD/Muslims
91	Malachi 1:11					134	LD/Muslims
92	Malachi 3:1	33, 94-101	Muhammad			149,150	Muhammad
93	Matt. 3:11,12	145-163	Muhammad				
94	Matt. 10:23					15	Muhammad
95	Matt. 11:11	157-158	Muhammad				
96	Matt. 13:43					53,130	LD/Muslims
97	Matt. 21:42					87	Islam/Ka'ba
98	Matt. 21:43			M11	Islam/Muslims		
99	Matt. 22:41-46	59	Muhammad			38	Muhammad
100	Matt. 24:15-21					133	LD/Muslims
101	Matt. 25:34,41					130	LD/Muslims
102	Mark 13:14					141	LD/Muslims
103	Luke 2:14	125-134, 140-144	Islam/Muhammad				
104	Luke 3:16,17	145-163, 175-184	Islam				

	Bible	Abd al-Ahad Dawood		Ahmeed Hoosen Deedat		Abdurahim Baymatov	
105	Luke 7:28	157-158	Muhammad				
106	Luke 24:49	139	Muhammad				
107	John 1:15	158, 159	Muhammad				
108	John 1:25	147-148	Muhammad	W21,22	Muhammad	15	Muhammad
109	John 5:33,35	164-165	Muhammad				
110	John 14:16,26	139, 192, 202	Muhammad	M21	Muhammad	92,93	Muhammad/Islam
111	John 15:26	139, 192, 202	Muhammad	M21	Muhammad	92,93	
112	John 16:7	139	Muhammad	M15,21	Muhammad		
113	John 16:8,9	203	Muhammad			92	Muhammad
114	John 16:13	205	Muhammad	M26,27, 39	Muhammad		
115	1Thess. 4:16,17					37	LD/Muslims
116	Hebrews 7:22					9	Islam
117	Hebrews 8:6					9	Islam
118	Hebrews 12:25-29					9	Islam
119	Rev. 1:16					54	Islam
120	Rev. 2:7,11,17					151	LD/Muslims
121	Rev. 2:26-28					129,151	LD/Muslims
122	Rev. 3:4-5					151	LD/Muslims
123	Rev. 3:12					30,151	LD/Muslims
124	Rev. 3:18					155	Islam/LD
125	Rev. 3:21					129,151	LD/Muslims
126	Rev. 4:7					12	Islam
127	Rev. 5:9					7,12, 154	Qur'an
128	Rev. 6:6-17					69,153	LD/Muslims
129	Rev. 7:1-3					52	Islam
130	Rev. 7:9-17					53,131	LD/Muslims

	Bible	Abd al-Ahad Dawood	Ahmeed Hoosen Deedat	Abdurahim Baymatov	
131	Rev. 8:3-5			135	LD/Islam
132	Rev. 8:13			67	LD/Muhammad
133	Rev. 9:13-16			31,134	LD/Muslims
134	Rev. 10:1-7			53	Islam
135	Rev. 11:1,2			135	LD/Muslims
136	Rev. 12:1,2			50	Islam
137	Rev. 12:6,7			22	Islam/Muslims
138	Rev. 12:14-17			12	Islam
139	Rev. 13:1-3			68	LD
140	Rev. 13:1-10			132	LD/Muslims
141	Rev. 13:17-18			24-25, 69-70	LD
142	Rev. 14:1-3			7	Qur'an
143	Rev. 15:2,3			14,160	LD/Qur'an/Muslims
144	Rev. 15:1-8			69	LD/Qur'an
145	Rev. 16:8-9			52	Islam
146	Rev. 16:1-10			70	LD/Muslims
147	Rev. 16:12			31,49,134	LD/Muslims
148	Rev. 19:11-21			38	LD/Muhammad
149	Rev. 19:17-18			53	Islam
150	Rev. 21:7			152	LD/Muslims

The Real Story Behind the Massacre of the Banu Qurayza

Daniel Janosik

Abstract

Muslims today look to Muhammad as their perfect model for life. Their sharia law is largely based on what Muhammad supposedly did and said. However, some of the actions attributed to Muhammad seem to be embarrassing to Muslims today because they cannot reconcile Muhammad's supposed deeds with their estimation of a perfect model. One of these controversial incidents is the massacre of the Jewish tribe called the Banu Qurayza, where Islamic history records the death of over 600 Jewish men at the hands of Muhammad in one day. The first Muslim biographer, Ibn Ishaq (d.767) narrates the story in great detail and makes Muhammad out to be the hero, but Muslims today are uncomfortable with their prophet being portrayed as a murderer, so they tend to overlook the incident, cover it up or re-interpret the events. However, if Ibn Ishaq is to be trusted as a recorder of the life of Muhammad, then he should have the last word in this account as well.

This article recounts the events leading up to the massacre. The first part explains the supposed problems Muhammad had with two Jewish tribes, the Qaynuqa and the Al Nadir, and his banishment of them. This sets the stage for his later judgment of a third Jewish tribe, the Banu Qurayza. The Battle of the Trench is an important event leading up Muhammad's dealings with the Banu Qurayza, so this battle is covered as Ibn Ishaq relates it. Nothing much happens with the battle against the Medinans, but Muhammad is able to use it to instigate his men to go up against the last remaining Jewish obstacle remaining in Medina. After a month-long siege, the men of the Banu Qurayza surrender to Muhammad expecting to be banished as the two tribes before them. However, they learn to their horror, as they are led out in small groups to another trench dug for their graves, that their punishment would be death at the hands of Muhammad. Even if all the charges of rebellion against them were true, this punishment did not seem justified. Even today Muslims find it hard to justify Muhammad's actions, but if Ibn Ishaq is correct in his narration, then both Muslims and non-Muslims need to know the details of this story in order to better understand Muhammad and the origins of Islam.

Introduction: The Jewish Problem

If the Jews of Medina had known how shrewd a strategist Muhammad was, they probably would have put up more of a resistance. However, by the time they began to understand his true purpose, it was too late. Two tribes, the Banu Qaynuqa and the Banu Al Nadir were besieged and then expelled from the city. The Banu Qurayza were not as fortunate. They were hoping for banishment, but instead they received death, at least for the 700 or so fighting men among them. Why was Muhammad's judgment so harsh? Why could he not tolerate these Jewish tribes living among the growing Muslim population? And how did this fit into his overall strategy?

At first, when Muhammad came to Yathrib (later renamed "Medina," or city of the prophet), he sought support from the Jews and considered them to be "people of the book."

> Ibn Ishaq shows us that the Jews actually permitted Muhammad to participate in the activities of their community during the first few months after his arrival in Medina. The scenario presented by Ibn Ishaq shows Muhammad pass sentence on a Jewish couple, raise the value of the blood price of the B. Qurayza to equal that of the B. Nadir and become involved in religious arguments with them. It suggests an atmosphere of integration and active proselytizing that is barely visible in the al-Waqidi text. Ibn Ishaq suggests that the better moments had encouraged Muhammad to believe that the Jews could be included in an Umma with the Muslims. Unfortunately, the activity led to much religious conflict... and... Jewish rejection of Muhammad.[1]

He never did force them to convert to Islam, as he did the pagans, but he soon realized that if he were going to fulfill his empire-building plans for Medina and Arabia, the resistant Jews were going to have to go.[2] Wellhausen points out at least three stages in this

---

[1] Rizwi Faizer, *Ibn Ishak and Al-Waqidi Revisited: A Case Study of Muhammad and the Jews in Bibliographical Literature* (McGill University Doctoral Thesis), 171.

[2] John Glubb, *The Life and Times of Muhammad* (Chelsea, MI: Scarborough House Publishers, 1970), 221.

"drama." First there was the "acceptance stage" where Muhammad "had orientated himself on their religion, had repeatedly tried to win them over – but without avail." He had even oriented the qibla, or the direction of prayer towards Jerusalem, perhaps in the hope of winning over some of the Jews or at least linking Islam to Abraham and the accepted religions of Judaism and Christianity. Later, however, almost as a symbolic gesture of his change of opinion toward the Jews, seventeen or eighteen months after Muhammad's arrival in Medina he changed the qibla towards Mecca.[3] Apparently the treatment he had received from the Jews, rejection as a true prophet and political leader, had continued to feed his anger and frustration, but at the same time had to be restrained until the time was right.[4] He came to realize that if he were going to "achieve his ideal, the establishment of a theocratic monarchy at Medina… his field of operation had to be cleared first."[5] He had to get rid of the Jews.[6] At the heart of his plan was the formation of a new umma, or society, that in effect would transcend the political limitations tribal affiliation generated among the Arabs. Keshk comments that "the problem for Muhammad was not that they were Jewish; the problem was that they remained tribal, and they remained for the most part antagonistic towards him."[7] Since they would not relent to his political entreaties, the Jews had to be dealt with. According to Keshk, the problem was that,

> the three Jewish tribes of Medina were so adapted to their local environment and were deeply rooted in tribal traditions and customs that they could not accept or compromise with the new umma or the state that this umma was molding. The confrontation came because the Jews rejected Muhammad as an arbiter and not as a prophet, even though they had done both.[8]

---

[3] Faizer, *Ibn Ishak and Al-Waqidi Revisited*, 171.

[4] Julius Wellhausen, *Muhammad and the Jews of Medina* (trans. A.J. Weinsinck, Freiburg: K. Shwarz, 1975), 105.

[5] Wellhausen, *Muhammad and the Jews of Medina*, 105.

[6] Wellhausen, *Muhammad and the Jews of Medina*, 105.

[7] Khaled Muhammad Galal Muhammad Ali Keshk, *The Conflict between Muhammad and the Three Jewish Tribes of Medina* (Dept. of Languages, University of Utah Master's Thesis, December 1987), 67.

[8] Keshk, *The Conflict between Muhammad and the Three Jewish Tribes of Medina*, 67-68.

Keshk portrays only part of the story, however. The umma was very much a political concept,[9] but it was also the basis of his budding theocracy. As the Jews continued to reject him as the prophet of the new umma, he knew that he would need to do something about their resistance. Wellhausen suggests that

> Muhammad had long realized that he could not achieve his ideal, the establishment of a theocratic monarchy at Medina, so long as he was surrounded by a party which almost equaled his own disciples numerically, upon whom he could not count, and who he previously had to fear. Thus, his field of operation had to be cleared first.[10]

Muhammad's earlier treatment of the Jews was, therefore, merely part of the means by which he could attain his own goal. Wellhausen points out that Muhammad only had to wait "until his position had become sufficiently established so as not to need them any longer."[11] The purpose of getting the Jews to agree to the Constitution of Medina and his earlier friendly treatment of the Jewish tribes was, perhaps, all part of biding his time. Later, the banishment of the two tribes and the massacre of the Banu Qurayza were necessary in order for Muhammad to become the *de facto* leader of Medina, and later of all Arabia. The tribal ties had to be eliminated in order for the new umma to rise up and create a greater loyalty to a greater cause.[12] This became part of an unfolding plan.

Early Opportunities and the Expulsion of the Qaynuqa

Muhammad's first major opportunity to remove "liability groups," such as the Jews, came with the Battle of Badr. The earlier raids had brought funds into the coffers and men into the new umma, but Muhammad needed more legitimacy in the eyes of the Meccans and a greater call to destiny for his ideals. Thus, even though the actual military results of Badr were insignificant, the psychological repercussions were far-reaching. Wellhausen writes,

> Muhammad's prestige was considerably increased in all of Arabia, and his position at Medina put on solid foundation. The rest of the

---

[9] Serjeant, *The Sunnah Jamiah Pact*, 154.

[10] Wellhausen, *Muhammad and the Jews of Medina*, 105.

[11] Wellhausen, *Muhammad and the Jews of Medina*, 104.

[12] Keshk, *The Conflict between Muhammad and the Three Jewish Tribes of Medina*, 68.

polytheists could probably in no way be converted more quickly than by Muhammad's success and the expectation of booty and honour in war. The Jews were weakened; they felt humiliated and disappointed now that the abused prophet had shown himself as a man of insight and energy in the eyes of Arabia.[13]

Even though the battle was against the Meccans, the Jews in Medina would have felt the repercussions early on. Immediately after his success over the Meccans, Muhammad capitalized on his victory and turned his eyes toward the Jews. They were an obstacle to his plans, but they also could provide some of his material needs through their property, houses and livestock. His followers, especially the ones who came from Mecca, had very few possessions and a number of them were living on charity.[14] Houses and lands would be a great reward and motivation for continued loyalty. He started, therefore, with the Qaynuqa because they were the weakest of the three main tribes and they lived the closest. He probably also realized that he would need to take one tribe at a time. Muhammad used the excuse that they had broken their agreement with the Muslims. It even seems that he had a revelation that prompted him to take action against them: "If you fear treachery from any people cancel [the agreement] in the like manner; Allah hates deceivers."[15] In only 15 days the Qaynuqa were prisoners in the hands of the Muslims. Wellhausen believes that, based on Al-Waqidi and Ibn Ishaq, it was Muhammad's intention to kill his captives.[16] It was only after Ibn Salul stepped in and besought Muhammad to spare their lives that he finally relented.[17] Perhaps he thought that banishment would still serve his purpose in removing the obstacle and providing material comforts for his men. Whatever his real motives were for sparing the Qaynuqa, their expulsion brought him greater respect and a more

---

[13] Wellhausen, *Muhammad and the Jews of Medina*, 105.

[14] Glubb, *The Life and Times of Muhammad*, 198.

[15] Qur'an, Sura 8:60.

[16] Glubb, *The Life and Times of Muhammad*, 108.

[17] Muhammad Ibn Ishaq, *The Life of Muhammad*, ed. Alfred Guillaume (Karachi: Oxford University Press, 1955), 363.

solid position militarily. Soon it would be time to deal with the next Jewish tribe, the Al Nadir.

The Banishment of the Al Nadir

Getting the true story behind the reason for the expulsion of the Al Nadir is not easy. The traditional reason given by Ibn Ishaq is that after having agreed to pay blood-money for two men of Beni Aamir, Muhammad went to the Jewish tribe of Al Nadir to seek funds to help in the settlement, apparently something that was commonly done in that time. The Jews agreed to help, but as they sought counsel privately among themselves they determined that this would be an ideal time to kill Muhammad and be rid of his growing influence. One man, Amr ibn Jahash, agreed to go up to the roof and drop a large stone on the Apostle. However, Muhammad found out about the plot and hastily retreated to Medina while some of his men waited, unaware of his departure. Muhammad then returned with his followers in order to make war on the al Nadir. Some say that the plot was overheard while Ibn Ishaq indicates that Muhammad received a warning from heaven.[18] In September of 625 AD/4 AH,[19] after a siege of less than three weeks, the Al Nadir surrendered on the condition that they would be allowed to emigrate to Syria. Muhammad agreed and the Muslims confiscated the houses, lands and weapons of the Jews.[20] Wensinck indicates that one of the reasons that Muhammad went up against the Al Nadir was because they were a wealthy tribe and had considerable land-holdings. "It is no surprise that such property caused the envy of Muhammad, especially since he and his followers were dependant upon their fellow-townsmen, and because the muhajirun lived in poor circumstances."[21] Wellhausen also points out the advantages accrued to Muhammad with the departure of the Al Nadir:

> Extensive land became vacant which was distributed among the Muhajirun. Also the number of his opponents diminished noticeably

---

[18] Ibn Ishaq, *The Life of Muhammad*, 437-438.

[19] Glubb, *The Life and Times of Muhammad*, 224.

[20] Glubb, *The Life and Times of Muhammad*, 224.

[21] Wellhausen, *Muhammad and the Jews of Medina*, 26.

which in turn curtailed the power of the munafiqun. Muhammad and his party no longer had to fear any strong resistance in Medina. The theocracy had become the only power and manifested itself in various expeditions which were launched.[22]

From a different angle, McDonald seeks to answer the question of why Muhammad attacked the al-Nadir. He says that the underlying cause "was the same as in the case of Qaynuqa, namely that Jewish criticisms endangered the ordinary Muslim's belief in Muhammad's prophethood and in the Qur'an as revelation from God. It should be kept in mind that the attack was made only a few weeks after the Muslim loss of life at al-Raji and Bi'r Ma'unah (where 40 Muslims were killed)".[23] Thus, McDonald feels that this attack was made to revive Muslim confidence and shore up flagging spirits due to the recent disappointments brought about by the reversals at Uhud, al-Raji and Bi'r Ma'una. He claims, therefore, that the "story about someone in Nadir plotting to drop a stone on Muhammad's head was probably just a pretext if not a later invention."[24] Whatever the reason, another group of detractors was gone and Muhammad's new umma was growing, not only in numbers but also in confidence. The Al Nadir had said that they would depart for Syria, and while many did emigrate to Syria, a number of others went north to Khaybar to join forces with the Jews there.[25] In time this would lead to a greater concern for Muhammad, for, as Wellhausen puts it, "together with the native Jewish population, they represented a formidable power which could exert considerable influence upon the events in the Hijaz. Medina was far from safe, hard-pressed by Mecca in the south and Khaybar in the north. Thus, it was not long until there was an attack."[26] Muhammad would not make the mistake again of letting such a large force leave only to become part of a greater opposition. The fate of the Banu Qurayza was already locking itself into place. There was only one more major piece to be put on the board, the Battle of the Trench.

---

[22] Wellhausen, *Muhammad and the Jews of Medina*, 121-122.

[23] McDonald, Vol. 7 Al-Tabari, xxxv.

[24] McDonald, Vol. 7 Al-Tabari, xxxvi.

[25] Wellhausen, *Muhammad and the Jews of Medina*, 122.

[26] Wellhausen, *Muhammad and the Jews of Medina*, 122.

The Battle of the Trench (Khandaq)

After the battle of Uhud, the leader of the Quraysh army, Abu Sufyan, had called for a "rematch" to take place a year later in Badr. Halfway to Badr, however, Abu Safyan decided that the conditions were not right and turned back. Apparently, because of the abnormally dry conditions there was not enough food for the horses. When Muhammad and his men arrived at Badr his opponents were nowhere to be seen. They remained camped out for 8 nights before they decided to return.[27] Even though no battle took place, Muhammad and his men were greatly encouraged and began to see themselves as morally and militarily superior to the old order.[28]

Within a year, however, the Quraysh began putting together another army to try to crush the growing threat of the Muslim blockades against the Meccan trading caravans en route to Syria. Ibn Ishaq claims that some of the Jews from Khaybar were responsible for instigating the Meccans and Bedouin tribes like the Ghatafan to put an end to Muhammad and his followers once and for all.[29] Wellhausen discusses the efforts depicted in the Muslim sources by Huyayy ibn Akhtab to convince the leader of the Jewish Qurayzah in Medina, Ka'b ibn Asad, to break their treaty with Muhammad and join the Meccan confederation preparing to attack Medina.

> Evidently Qurayzah decided only hesitantly to terminate the good understanding they had with Muhammad. Already during the siege they had refused to support al-Nadir. Therefore it was not easy for Huyayy ibn Akhtab to persuade Ka'b ibn Asad because to take sides for or against Muhammad was a matter of life and death. If after their defection Yathrib was not conquered and captured by Quraysh, the destruction of the Jews was certain.[30]

It is clear from the older sources that the Jews did not take part in the siege of Khandaq.[31] The Jews broke their treaty with

---

[27] Ibn Ishaq, *The Life of Muhammad*, 447.

[28] Ibn Ishaq, *The Life of Muhammad*, 448.

[29] Ibn Ishaq, *The Life of Muhammad*, 450.

[30] Wellhausen, *Muhammad and the Jews of Medina*, 122-123.

[31] Ibn Ishaq, *The Life of Muhammad*, 450-457.

Muhammad but did not actively support the Meccans. Wellhausen calls this, "certainly the least advantageous attitude they could have adopted".[32]

When Muhammad received the news of the "grand alliance" assembled against the Muslims he sought counsel with his leaders. This time they decided not to fight out in the open as they had done at Uhud. That would mean certain defeat, especially since the Quraysh alliance forces were 10,000 strong to Muhammad's 3,000.[33] The Muslims were fortunate to have with them a convert who came from a Christian background in Syria and, after a number of misfortunes, became a fervent follower of Muhammad. He was the one who came up with the idea of digging a trench around the exposed part of the city.[34] This proved easier to build than a wall. In fact, within 6 days of hard labor the ditch was finished. From estimates given by Ahmad Barakat, the ditch ran from Shaykhayn to the Mount of Banu Ubayd, a distance of over 2 km.[35] Others say that it only filled in the gaps between the houses.[36]

The confederacy led by the Quraysh began to arrive in early February of 627 AD (5 AH).[37] The Qur'an describes the situation as follows: "When they come against you from above [referring to the Banu Qurayza] and from below you [referring to the Meccans and Bedouins], and when your eyes swerved and your hearts reached your throats, while you thought thoughts about God; there it was that the believers were tried, and shaken most mightily."[38] Indeed, with the Meccans before him and the Banu Qurayza behind him, Muhammad was in a precarious position. If the Jews had decided to attack, it could have been the end of Muhammad and the Muslims. However, they chose to wait and watch. In the end, the

---

[32] Wellhausen, *Muhammad and the Jews of Medina*, 123.

[33] Ibn Ishaq, *The Life of Muhammad*, 452.

[34] Glubb, *The Life and Times of Muhammad*, 243-244.

[35] Ahmad Barakat, *Muhammad and the Jews,* (New Delhi: Vikas Publishing House, 1979), 68.

[36] Glubb, *The Life and Times of Muhammad*, 245.

[37] Barakat, *Muhammad and the Jews*, 68; Ibn Ishaq, *The Life of Muhammad,* 450.

[38] Qur'an, Sura 33: 10-11.

ditch proved to be a divide that could not be breached and after 27 days of small skirmishes and volleys of arrows, the confederacy had enough of Muhammad's war that brought no honor[39] and left suddenly in the early morning. The retreat was no doubt hastened by the cold wind which overturned their cooking pots and upset their once-determined spirits.[40] Perhaps they realized that they were up against a new type of force that they were not prepared to conquer. Glubb says that,

> If there were any difference in the fighting performance of the two sides, it was in the sphere of morale rather than in that of physical courage. Quraysh were waging a negative and, therefore, an uninspiring war. They did not want changes introduced into their way of life. The Muslims, on the other hand, were fired by the positive conviction that God had entrusted to them the task of reforming the world. It was in the spirit which inspired them that the two sides differed.[41]

Perhaps the Jewish tribes in Medina also made the mistake of clinging to a past that was quickly blowing away with the strong winds whipping across the desert. Muhammad was that wind, and the new ummah he was creating was the sand that would reshape much of the world as it swept across many lands and into many lives. On a different front, Watt has observed that the Banu Qurayza could have brought about the demise of Muhammad and his forces, but in the end they did not fight.[42] Perhaps their hesitancy to act brought about their own demise.

What Really Happened to the Banu Qurayza?

In March of the year 627 AD (5 AH),[43] after the Quraysh retreated back to Mecca and the Battle of the Trench was over, Muhammad and his 3,000 men turned their efforts toward the Banu Qurayza.

---

[39] Glubb, *The Life and Times of Muhammad*, 244.

[40] Ibn Ishaq, *The Life of Muhammad*, 460.

[41] Glubb, *The Life and Times of Muhammad*, 248.

[42] W. Montgomery Watt, *Muhammad at Medina* (Oxford: Clarendon Press, 1956), 39.

[43] Wellhausen, *Muhammad and the Jews of Medina*, 126.

After laying siege to their fortress for 25 days[44] the Banu Qurayza surrendered unconditionally, apparently hoping for the same sentence as two other Jewish tribes from the Medina area: banishment. However, Muhammad now had the power to make a bolder stroke and leave a more powerful impression. At the end of the next day, 600 -900 males were beheaded and dumped into another ditch and the women and children were taken as property and many were later sold into slavery in exchange for weapons and horses.[45]

According to Ibn Ishaq, after it was discovered that the enemy had departed, "the apostle and the Muslims left the trench and returned to Medina, laying their arms aside."[46] Muhammad realized the opportunity he now had to further his plan of shifting the loyalty of the people away from the tribes and towards the new universal ummah, that of Islam. The Jewish tribe of the Banu Qurayza were one of the major obstacles to the realization of that goal and now was the time to do something about it. Ibn Ishaq records that as Muhammad was making his way back from the battle-line Gabriel came to him and urged him not to rest but rather continue the battle on a different front:

> According to what al-Zuhri told me, at the time of the noon prayers Gabriel came to the apostle wearing an embroidered turban and riding on a mule with a saddle covered with a piece of brocade. He asked the apostle if he had abandoned fighting, and when he said that he had he said that the angels had not yet laid aside their arms and that he had just come from pursuing the enemy. 'God commands you, Muhammad, to go to B. Qurayza. I am about to go to them to shake their stronghold.'[47]

It is interesting to note that when Muhammad asked some bystanders if they had also seen the rider on the mule with a saddle covered with a piece of brocade they replied that they had seen a certan Dihya b. Khalifa al-Kalbi upon a white mule fitting that description. Muhammad was quick to assure them that it was really

---

[44] Ibn Ishaq, *The Life of Muhammad*, 461.

[45] Ibn Ishaq, *The Life of Muhammad*, 464.

[46] Ibn Ishaq, *The Life of Muhammad*, 460.

[47] Ibn Ishaq, *The Life of Muhammad*, 461. See also al-Bukhari, *Volume 4, Book 52, Number 6*.

the angel Gabriel,48 but how could we verify that? And why would Gabriel reveal himself to others when Muhammad was the only one who ever experienced his presence? Perhaps Muhammad was using this incident to give a spiritual basis for something that he had determined in his own heart.

Ibn Ishaq continues, 'The prophet ordered it to be announced that none should perform the afternoon prayer until after he reached B. Qurayza. The apostle sent 'Ali forward with his banner and the men hastened to it.'49 One modern historian mentions that since some men did not perform their afternoon prayers until after their evening prayers that the trip from Medina to the village housing the Banu Qurayza must have taken four or five hours, but even on the map that he includes in his book the distance is shown as less than 2 km!50 Surely it would not take four or five hours to walk that distance (a little over 1 mile)! When Muhammad and his men finally arrived Ibn Ishaq reports that, 'The apostle besieged them for twenty-five nights until they were sore pressed and God cast terror into their hearts.'51

During the seige Ibn Ishaq relates how Huyayy b. Akhtab from the Al Nadir tribe, who had been banished previously, returned in order to fulfill his promise to the B. Qurayza. When they felt certain that Muhammad was not going to lift his blockade, Ka`b b. Asad surmised the situation and supposedly outline their three possibilities: 1) accept Muhammad as a prophet and agree to follow him, 2) kill their women and children and fight the Muslims to their death, or 3) try to take Muhammad and his men by surprise on the Sabbath.52 The Jews did not want to accept Muhammad, even if it meant their death, and they felt even more strongly about killing their own women and children, for then there would be nothing left to fight for.53 I am not sure why they did not consider further the

---

[48] Ibn Ishaq, *The Life of Muhammad*, 461.

[49] Ibn Ishaq, *The Life of Muhammad*, 461.

[50] Barakat, *Muhammad and the Jews*, 69, 84.

[51] Ibn Ishaq, *The Life of Muhammad*, 461.

[52] Ibn Ishaq, *The Life of Muhammad*, 461.

[53] Ibn Ishaq, *The Life of Muhammad*, 462.

idea of a surprise attack on the Sabbath, for surely it was better than wasting away. Perhaps they were confident that Muhammad would find banishment a favorable sentence and at that point the loss of their houses and lands did not rate in the same category as saving their lives.

One of the questions that surfaces is how the Muslims would have known about these deliberations made behind the fortified walls of the Banu Qurayza so that later biographers such as Ibn Ishaq could include it in his narrative. Could these deliberations have merely been words placed in the mouths of the Jews, as is often done in order to shed a more favorable light on the Muslims and their Prophet?[54] Or could they at least contain a kernel of truth since the Jews knew that their lives were on the line? One phrase from the account does seem to prefigure the ultimate action of Muhammad, and the consequent sense of doom on the part of the Jews: "the apostle would not leave them until he had made an end of them."[55] Would there still be hope of banishment?

The Jews ask for a trusted ally, Abu Lubaba b. `Abdu'l-Mundhir, to arbitrate a surrender for them, but when Abu Lubaba met with them his judgment that they should submit to Muhammad was accompanied with a gesture to his throat signifying slaughter.[56] Apparently Lubaba, who genuinely felt sorry for the plight of his friends, was so overcome with this divulgence of Muhammad's plan that he ran to the mosque and lashed himself to one of the pillars saying that he was not going to leave until Allah forgave him for what he had done.[57] Fortunately for him, Muhammad received a revelation in the morning that Abu Lubaba had been forgiven by Allah.[58]

---

[54] Wellhausen, *Muhammad and the Jews of Medina*, 123. Wellhausen often questions the probability of certain sayings when they show themselves to be highly improbable and conveniently slanted.

[55] Ibn Ishaq, *The Life of Muhammad*, 461.

[56] Ibn Ishaq, *The Life of Muhammad*, 462.

[57] Ibn Ishaq, *The Life of Muhammad*, 462.

[58] Ibn Ishaq, *The Life of Muhammad*, 462-463.

That same morning Ka'b b. Asad and the rest of the Banu Qurayza surrendered to Muhammad and cast themselves to his mercy. Al-Aus, an ally of the Banu Qurayza leapt up and tried to persuade Muhammad to merely banish the Jews as he had done with the B. Qaynuqa and the al-Nadir, but it seems that Muhammad had already made up his mind. It is important to remember that when Abdullah b. Ubayy b. Salul urged Muhammad to spare the Qaynuqa that Muhammad got angry with him and it was only with great persistence that Salul was able to appease Muhammad and obtain a life-saving order of expulsion for the Jews.[59] It is also important to note that Wellhausen has argued that it was Muhammad's original intention to kill the Banu Qaynuqa when they surrendered.[60] This may help us understand Muhammad's next move of asking the Aus if they would be satisfied to submit to the judgment of one of their own leaders. After they agree he names Sa'd b. Mu'adh as the one who would determine the fate of the Banu Qurayza.[61] Ibn Ishaq indicates that it is Muhammad who chooses Sa'd for the job. Later writers, perhaps trying to wrench any of the responsibility of the massacre out of Muhammad's hand, argue that it was the Banu Qurayza themselves who asked for Sa'd to be their arbitrator.[62] The choice of Sa'd b. Mu'adh was a shrewd move on the part of Muhammad. It would not only remove the burden of the ultimate responsibility off of Muhammad's shoulders, but it would also prevent the Aus from applying too much pressure so that he would have to relent and let the Jews face only expulsion as had happened with the Qaynuqa previously. Ultimately, the destiny of the Jews had already been sealed with the selection of Sa'd because of his previous unpleasant experiences with the Banu Qurayza.[63] Wellhausen adds, "That the Prophet appointed Sa'd ibn Mu'adh as judge is not objectionable for the older biographers. He

---

[59] Ibn Ishaq, *The Life of Muhammad*, 363.

[60] Wellhausen, *Muhammad and the Jews of Medina*, 104.

[61] Ibn Ishaq, *The Life of Muhammad*, 463.

[62] Ibn Kathir, *al-Sira al-Nabawiyya*, 463, cited in Keshk, *The Conflict between Muhammad and the Three Jewish Tribes of Medina*, 64. Also see Wellhausen, *Muhammad and the Jews of Medina*, 125; also found in al-Bukari, *Volume 8, Book 74, Number 278*.

[63] Wellhausen, *Muhammad and the Jews of Medina*, 125.

was an Aus, the most respected Aus of the time. What better man could Muhammad have chosen?"[64]

Who Was Sa'd b. Mu'adh?

What do we know about Sa'd b. Mu'adh? And why did Muhammad choose this particular leader? Ibn Ishaq writes that when Muhammad sent Sa'd to test the loyalty of Ka'b b. Asad and the Banu Qurayza to the agreement that they had made with Muhammad, Sa'd showed that he was a man with a "hasty temper" and sought vengeance against the Jews for what he felt were disparaging words against the prophet.[65] We see this anger against the Jews in a number of other instances as well. For example, after the Battle of Badr,

> The foe was routed. God slew many of their chiefs and made captive many of their nobles. Meanwhile the apostle was in the hut and Sa'd b. Mu'adh was standing at the door of the hut girt with his sword. With him were some of the Ansar guarding the apostle for fear lest the enemy should come back at him. While the folk were laying hands on the prisoners the apostle, as I have been told, saw displeasure on the face of Sa'd at what they were doing. He said to him, 'You seem to dislike what the people were doing.' 'Yes, by God,' he replied, 'it is the first defeat that God has brought on the infidel and I would rather see them slaughtered than left alive.'[66]

This seems to indicate that Sa'd does not like the idea of having any prisoners. His desire is to see them all killed. Muhammad noted Sa'd's attitude at that time and probably tucked it away for further use.

In another incident, Aisha had been accused of immorality and after she was exonerated and the false accusers discovered, Muhammad came to her defense. In this Hadith we also learn a little more about the loyalty of Sa'd bin Mu'adh and his readiness to shed the blood of anyone who would cast doubt on Muhammad and his family.

Narrated 'Aisha: ...

---

[64] Wellhausen, *Muhammad and the Jews of Medina*, 125.

[65] Ibn Ishaq, *The Life of Muhammad*, 453.

[66] Ibn Ishaq, *The Life of Muhammad*, 301.

So, on that day, Allah's Apostle got up on the pulpit and complained about 'Abdullah bin Ubai (bin Salul) before his companions, saying, 'O you Muslims! Who will relieve me from that man who has hurt me with his evil statement about my family? By Allah, I know nothing except good about my family and they have blamed a man about whom I know nothing except good and he used never to enter my home except with me.' Sa'd bin Mu'adh the brother of Banu 'Abd Al-Ashhal got up and said, 'O Allah's Apostle! I will relieve you from him; if he is from the tribe of Al-Aus, then I will chop his head off, and if he is from our brothers, i.e. Al-Khazraj, then order us, and we will fulfill your order.'[67]

After Sa'd was mortally wounded by an arrow striking the medial artery of his forearm during the Battle of the Trench, he made a comment that showed his true attitude toward the Jews: "O God, seeing that you have appointed war between us and them grant me martyrdom and do not let me die until I have seen my desire upon B. Qurayza."[68]

In time he would die from the wound, but not before Muhammad gave him the opportunity to have his "desire" manifested upon the Banu Qurayza. Surely Muhammad knew the mind of Sa'd and his disdain for the Jews of Banu Qurayza. Could this be the reason that Muhammad chose Sa'd b. Mu'adh for the role of judge? It would be a brilliant move. The Aus would not object because Sa'd was well-respected among them. Also, they could not refute Muhammad's choice of judge since they had previously agreed to accept his choice beforehand.[69] The judgment from someone other than Muhammad would also remove the ultimate culpability from Muhammad himself and he could therefore distance himself from the criticism of not only his present enemies but also from future historians.

Finally Sa'd was called for and came from the mosque where Muhammad had someone taking care of his wounds. The Aus entreated him to act kindly upon the Banu Qurayza, but his reply was a preview of the sentence to come: "The time has come for

---

[67] Bukhari, Volume 5, Book 59, Number 462.

[68] Ibn Ishaq, *The Life of Muhammad*, 459.

[69] Ibn Ishaq, *The Life of Muhammad*, 463.

Sa'd in the cause of God, not to care for any man's censure."[70] With those words some already understood that the death sentence had already been pronounced upon the Banu Qurayza.[71] When Sa'd entered the room to give his judgment he first asked the Aus

> 'Do you covenant by Allah that you accept the judgment I pronounce on them?' They said Yes, and he said, 'And is it incumbent on the one who is here ?' (looking) in the direction of the apostle not mentioning him out of respect, and the apostle answered Yes. Sa'd said, 'Then I give judgment that the men should be killed, the property divided, and the women and children taken as captives.'[72]

Upon hearing these words Muhammad is quoted as saying, "You have given the judgment of Allah above the seven heavens."[73] It is interesting that he included Muhammad as an outsider in the decision process. This distancing may have been something that Muhammad desired since it would not implicate him as much in the gruesome events that would soon follow. In this way he could get away with the death of over 600 men and *the blame would ostensibly go to a dying man*.

Muhammad then had trenches dug in the market of Medina and sent for the men of Banu Qurayza in batches. Many may not have realized what was taking place because they kept asking Ka'b b. Asad "what he thought would be done with them. He replied, 'Will you never understand? Don't you see that the summoner never stops and those who are taken away do not return? By Allah it is death!' This went on until the apostle made an end of them."[74] The men would kneel beside the trench and some of Muhammad's men struck off their heads. In all between 600 and 900 men were brutally murdered. The women and children were sold into slavery and the houses and lands were divided up by the Prophet.[75] The Banu Qurayza no longer existed as a tribe.

---

[70] Ibn Ishaq, *The Life of Muhammad*, 463.

[71] Ibn Ishaq, *The Life of Muhammad*, 463.

[72] Ibn Ishaq, *The Life of Muhammad*, 464.

[73] Ibn Ishaq, *The Life of Muhammad*, 464.

[74] Ibn Ishaq, *The Life of Muhammad*, 464.

[75] Ibn Ishaq, *The Life of Muhammad*, 464. See also al-Bukhari, *Volume 5, Book 59, Number 362*.

As if to add insult to injury, as Muhammad was dividing the booty he retained the beautiful Jewess named Raihana bint Amr for himself. He desired to marry her, but she would not give up her faith and said to Muhammad, "Nay, leave me in your power, for that will be easier for me and for you."[76] The fact that Muhammad's men had just put her father, husband and relatives to death may have had something to do with her refusal to be married to the Prophet. Apparently Muhammad was displeased with her behavior, but he let her live and made her his concubine.[77] He seems to justify his action by the following verse:

> O Prophet! We allow thee thy wives whom thou hast dowered, and the slaves whom thy right hand possesseth out of the booty which God hath granted thee. [78]

Conclusion

Even if Sa'd b. Mu'adh was the one who pronounced the sentence of death upon the Banu Qurayza, it is understood in the Muslim world that Muhammad could have chosen to override Sa'd's judgment and exile the Jews as he had done in two previous cases. Thus, Muhammad is still responsible for the death of over 600 Jewish men. For many Muslims this conclusion is not acceptable. In this modern era of reconstructionist history, there are scholars who will go so far as to deny the historicity of an event in order to "rectify" history so that it will fit their own presuppositions, but in doing so they will have to deny the clear testimony of Ibn Ishaq, the first biographer of Muhammad. They can't have it both ways.

---

[76] Ibn Ishaq, *The Life of Muhammad*, 466.

[77] Ibn Ishaq, *The Life of Muhammad* 466.

[78] Qur'an, Sura 33:49.

Islam in Europe: Concerns, Trends and Debates

Peter Riddell

In 2009 a film entitled "The Demographic Problem" appeared on *YouTube*[1] and was circulated widely across the world, especially among the different churches. It used wide-ranging and detailed statistics to argue that Europe's aging population, together with the rapid growth of Muslim communities in Europe, would lead to Europe's demise. "In a matter of years, Europe, as we know it, will cease to exist," declared the film starkly, adding "Of all population growth in Europe since 1990, 90% has been Islamic immigration."[2]

A deconstruction of the film shows that the statistics quoted were unsourced and often inflated. Together with the sombre music that accompanied the narration, the film seemed designed to raise anxiety levels among its viewers. The film also addressed the situation in the United States and elsewhere in the world, and concluded with the statement that "some studies show that with Islam's current rate of growth, in five to seven years it will be the dominant religion of the world."

However, any critical review of such a film should not simply point out its weaknesses, but should also consider whether the film was raising issues that need discussion. Indeed, the sense of alarm captured by this film is reflected in diverse other ways in public discourse in Europe.

This paper will first consider the community concern arising from European demographic changes and the growth of Islamic minority communities in the continent. It will then examine evidence that will position us better to evaluate whether the sense of alarm captured by the film "The Demographic Problem" is merely unfounded hysteria or rather whether there is solid evidence of dramatic and irreversible social change taking place in Europe.

---

[1] http://www.youtube.com/watch?v=9atIjykihkc (29 October, 2010).

[2] No source was cited in support of this claim.

Non-Muslim Concerns and Debates

Poll Results

The sense of public concern in diverse Europe locations with the speed and degree of societal change is patently clear, and can be seen in the results of public opinion polls.

In a 2010 Poll presented in Berlin by the Friedrich Ebert Foundation for Political Education (FES), over 30 percent of respondents agreed that "foreigners come to abuse the welfare state." The statement that "one should send foreigners back home" in a limited job market attracted 31.7 percent support while 35.6 percent agreed that too many immigrants put Germany in danger of being "overrun". Although the above statements were couched in terms of immigration in general, the specific context that raised greatest concerns for poll respondents was where Islam was involved. Just over 58 percent of respondents said that "religious practice for Muslims in Germany should be seriously limited."[3]

Over the border in Austria, the Linz-based IMAS research group conducted a survey of a different format in 2010, in which 1,055 people were interviewed.[4] They were asked to rate a series of words according to whether they saw them in positive terms. The results were as follows:

Term	Percentage rating it positively
"safety"	69%
"justice"	65%
"order"	61%
"work"	56%
"multicultural"	17%
"European Union"	15%
"Islam"	3%

In a somewhat similar survey, Swedish and Danish opinions on immigration and Islam were compared. Some 65 percent of Swedes

---

[3] http://www.thelocal.de/national/20101013-30455.html (26 October, 2010).

[4] http://www.austriantimes.at/news/General_News/2010-06-01/23876/Nuclear_energy_found_more_popular_with_Austrians_than_Islam (2 November, 2010).

saw immigration in positive terms, compared with 50 percent of Danes; while 20 percent of Swedes saw it in negative terms, compared with 42 percent of Danes. On Islam, 47 percent of Swedes commented that they **did not** see Islam as a problem for social cohesion, compared to just 18 percent of Danes who held this view.[5]

Meanwhile, in France, legislation was passed in the French parliament in mid-2010 banning the public wearing of full face veils. In spite of accusations of Islamophobia by opponents of this legislation, polls showed that it carried widespread public support. The French daily *Le Figaro*, in the heat of the debate prior to the passing of the legislation, reported on a survey by *TNS Sofres pour Europe 1*, that showed 64% support for a total or limited ban, with 33% supporting a ban throughout France and a further 31% preferring a ban in certain specified public places. Some 22% opposed the ban, preferring an awareness-raising campaign among the population concerned, while 10% considered that the French Government should not intervene at all.[6]

The debate about banning the burqa was a hot issue throughout 2010 across many nations of Europe, where similar popular support was in evidence. The new Dutch Coalition government which took power in late 2010 quickly held discussions about a burqa ban and stricter immigration laws, with reports appearing that some 70-80% of the Dutch population supported these Coalition accords on the points of immigration, integration and security.[7] Similarly Italy moved to ban the burqa after a government report ruled in favour of the proposed legislation, just weeks after the French ban.[8]

Politicians Show Disquiet

With such widespread popular public discomfort with rapid demographic change and associated Islamic issues, politicians

---

[5] http://islamineurope.blogspot.com/2010/09/swedes-vs-danes-opinion-on-islam.html#more (22 September, 2010)

[6] http://www.lefigaro.fr/flash-actu/2010/04/24/97001-20100424FILWWW00439-burqa-33-des-francais-pour-l-interdire.php (2 November, 2010).

[7] http://islamineurope.blogspot.com/2010/10/pvv-price-burqa-ban-stricter.html#more (2 October, 2010).

[8] http://www.geo.tv/10-10-2010/72660.htm (26 October, 2010).

across the continent inevitably reflected these trends. It is important to discern two tracks here: first, the concern among policy makers and security agents with the activities of radical Islamist groups and second, the broader discomfort with a purported relative lack of integration of Muslim minority communities per se, compared with other minority communities.

Regarding the former, in late 2010 the French parliament approved a bill to strip foreign-born criminals of their French nationality and expel European Union citizens for certain crimes, with a particular application to terrorism charges.[9]

But such measures were merely the tip of the iceberg of official discomfort with Muslim minority presence in Europe. Broader concerns were articulated in October 2010 by Angela Merkel, Chancellor of Germany, when she said in a speech that "the approach [to build] a multicultural [society] and to live side-by-side and to enjoy each other... has failed, utterly failed."[10]

Meanwhile, even left-leaning political voices were showing concern in Germany. Around the same time the head of Germany's center-left Social Democratic Party, Sigmar Gabriel, called for tougher integration measures in an interview with *Spiegel Online*. He said that Germany should get tough on immigrants who are unwilling to learn the language and integrate; while insisting that such immigrants should be supported, the German government and society should also make their own demands in return, said Gabriel.[11]

Though the wording of the statements by both Merkel and Gabriel were generalised, there was little doubt that the primary referent in such critiques was the Muslim minority community in Germany.

Further uncharacteristically robust comment from the Left on the topic of immigration came in the Netherlands, where Leftwing Green (GroenLinks) leader Femke Halsema commented that

---

[9] http://www.expatica.com/fr/news/local_news/french-mps-vote-to-strip-immigrant-criminals-of-citizenship_102664.html (26 October, 2010).

[10] http://www.bbc.co.uk/news/world-europe-11559451 (26 October, 2010).

[11] http://www.spiegel.de/international/germany/0,1518,druck-718627,00.html (22 September, 2010).

progressive politicians and thinkers should be more outspoken in criticising Islam, rather than too often accepting the pressure that radical Muslims put on the Islamic community.[12]

The most prominent case of a politician providing a channel for public concern about Islam was that of Dutch politician Geert Wilders, brought to trial on charges of inciting racial hatred against Muslims in October 2010, accused of describing Islam as a form of Nazism and of comparing the "fascist" Koran to Adolf Hitler's "Mein Kampf", which is banned in the Netherlands.

Politicians Take more Conciliatory Approaches

Of course such voices from political figures expressing concern and disquiet on the questions of immigration and Islam were not the only ones to be heard.

A series of cartoons depicting Muhammad, prophet of Islam, in uncomplimentary perspective was published by the Danish newspaper *Jyllands-Posten* on 30 September 2005. The riots that ensued around the world reflected feelings of bitterness among many Muslims towards Denmark as a whole, as well as impacting negatively on Denmark's exports to Muslim-majority countries. So from time to time, Danish political figures express feelings of regret for the cartoons episode. For example, in October 2010 Denmark's foreign minister met Egypt's top cleric to defuse tensions caused by the republication of the cartoons, and said that the hurt caused to Muslims from the cartoons was "very regrettable."[13]

Around the same time, while German Chancellor Merkel was expressing significant doubts about the policy of multiculturalism, other Government initiatives took a more conciliatory approach. For example, the German Education Minister Annette Schavan announced at a news conference a plan to establish and help fund departments for Islamic studies at three universities, a move aimed at assisting the integration of its four million Muslims. The centres, designed to educate a new generation of imams and students of

---

[12] http://www.nisnews.nl/public/121010_1.htm (13 October, 2010).

[13] http://www.google.com/hostednews/afp/article/ALeqM5iHQYEmMeoyje0Ew9kCv6h T1Axb2A?docId=CNG.9dd1a1176881e712993720a765eec626.ae1 (26 October, 2010).

Islam, are to be based at the universities of Tuebingen, Muenster and Osnabrueck.[14]

Meanwhile leading members of the German opposition Social Democrats and Greens advocated on behalf of Islam in Germany, in calling for it to be recognised by the state as a religious community, similar to Christianity and Judaism.[15]

Demographics: the present picture

So far in this paper we have focused upon concerns expressed by Europeans, both prominent figures and rank-and-file members of the population, with rapid demographic change through immigration and especially with the Islamic dimension to those immigration issues, especially in terms of a perceived lack of integration. What are we to make of those concerns? Is this simply a case of an Islamophobic beat-up, or mass hysteria, or are demographic trends in Europe and associated lack of integration likely to cause a significant redefinition of European societies in generations to come? We will now proceed to consider the growth of Islamic communities in Europe, using those particular communities as our focus in considering broader issues of immigration.

Muslim Minority Communities

Many European countries do not formally record sizes of minority communities according to religious affiliation. There are estimates available, based on various ways of counting, and the following table provides a rough guide as to the Islamic presence in many European countries.[16]

Country	Muslim community	As Percentage
France	6,000,000	9.6%
Netherlands	945,000	5.8%

---

[14] http://www.expatica.com/de/news/german-news/germany-to-set-up-three-islamic-study-centres-berlin_103076.html (26 October, 2010).

[15] http://www.thelocal.de/article.php?ID=30329&print=true (8 October, 2010).

[16] http://news.bbc.co.uk/2/hi/europe/4385768.stm#netherlands (16 August, 2009).

Denmark	270,000	5%
Austria	339,000	4.1%
Germany	3,000,000	3.6%
Britain	2,000,000	3%
Spain	1,000,000	2.3%
Italy	825,000	1.4%

The film "The Demographic Problem" asserted that Europe presently had a Muslim minority population of 52 million.[17] Such a figure would encompass all of Europe, not just the European Union, where a figure of 20-25 million is more likely. Nevertheless, what is significant is the rate of growth; some reports suggest that the Muslim population of Europe more than doubled in the 30 years up to 2009.[18] Furthermore, if Turkey were to be accepted into the European Union, then that country's 98% Muslim population of over 70 million would significantly alter the ratio between Muslim and non-Muslim Europeans.

Such figures only tell part of the story, of course. Muslim newcomers to European countries have tended to cluster in specific locations, especially in the cities, leading to certain cities having far higher percentages of Muslims in their populations than country-based percentages would suggest. It is difficult to get accurate figures for Muslim community size in the cities of Europe. The following table provides figures drawn from one source. They are at the upper end of estimates, but they nevertheless illustrate the main point of clustering:

| Marseilles | 25% | The Hague | 14.2% |
| Malmo | 25% | Utrecht | 13.2% |

---

[17] Possibly drawn from statistics mentioned by the German German Central Institute Islam Archive, mentioned at http://en.wikipedia.org/wiki/Islam_in_Europe (29 November, 2010).

[18] Adrian Michael, 'Muslim Europe: the demographic time bomb transforming our continent', *The Telegraph*, August 8, 2009.
http://www.telegraph.co.uk/news/worldnews/europe/5994047/Muslim-Europe-the-demographic-time-bomb-transforming-our-continent.html (16 August, 2009).

Amsterdam	24%	Rotterdam	13%
Stockholm	20%	Copenhagen	12.6%
Brussels	27-20%	Paris (centre)	7.38%
Moscow	16-20%	Antwerp	6.7%
Greater London	17%	Hamburg	6.4%
Birmingham	14.3%	Berlin	5.9%

A snapshot of social change in a European city is provided by the case of Antwerp. An Antwerp municipal research department report of February 2010 recorded that 36.1% of all Antwerp residents are of immigrant origin. Within this group the biggest group is people of North African origin (10.4%), followed by Western Europeans and West-Asians (5.4% each) and Eastern Europeans (5%). Some 46% of Antwerp residents are in their 20s; 48% of teens and 56% of children up to age nine are of immigrant origin.[19]

Mosques

The rapid growth of mosques and Muslim prayer halls in Europe in recent decades is clearly evident. One sources traces the growth in purpose-built mosques in Germany from three in 1990 to 159 in 2008.[20] The euromuslim.net website estimated mosque and prayer hall numbers in 2007 in various European countries as follows: France (1500), Britain (1500), Germany 1000, Netherlands (500), Belgium (350), Italy (260), and Spain (200).[21]

Growing the Islamic Presence in Europe

While growth of religious institutions and symbols such as mosques and Muslim clothing is a natural function of an expanding

---

[19] http://islamineurope.blogspot.com/2010/02/antwerp-56-of-children-of-immigrant.html (2 November, 2010).

[20] http://www.middle-east-online.com/english/?id=27616; http://www.telegraph.co.uk/news/worldnews/1555604/Huge-mosque-stirs-protests-in-Cologne.html (2 November, 2010).

[21] http://media3.washingtonpost.com/wp-dyn/content/graphic/2007/12/09/ GR2007120900022.gif (2 November, 2010).

community, it would be naive to suggest that no other factors lie behind the increasing visibility of the Muslim presence in Europe. Indeed, significant resources are being devoted to developing and consolidating the Islamic presence in various European locations.[22] This is key, as the sense of anxiety about Islamic growth felt in many quarters in Europe not only derives from what has happened, but is also closely connected with a perception of what may come to pass – whether that perception is accurate or not. We will therefore now consider evidence of Muslim groups expanding the Islamic presence in Europe.

Mosques

The rapid growth of mosque numbers in Europe in recent decades brings with it not merely Islamic minority presence but also at times visible Muslim missionary zeal.

Spain is a particular focus of Muslim efforts to consolidate the presence of Islam, especially relevant given the fact that the Spanish peninsula was under varying degrees of Muslim control for almost 800 years.

Once the heart of the Islamic kingdom of al-Andalus, there are reports of ambitious plans to recreate the city of Cordoba as a pilgrimage site for Muslims throughout Europe. Funds are being sought for the construction of a half-size replica of Cordoba's eighth century great mosque, with project planners looking for support to the governments of the United Arab Emirates and Kuwait, as well as Muslim organisations in Morocco and Egypt. Other big mosques are reportedly planned for Medina Azahara near Cordoba, Seville and Granada.[23]

Meanwhile in Germany, Cologne city council approved construction of a new US$20 million mosque in August 2008, with a capacity of 2,000 worshippers and twin minarets that will reach 170ft. The close proximity of this new mosque to Cologne cathedral

---

[22] See my study of Islamic *da'wa*: 'The Call to Islam: Diverse Methods and Varied Responses' Stuttgarter Theologische Themen V (2010) (forthcoming).

[23] http://www.independent.co.uk/news/world/europe/spanish-bishops-fear-rebirth-of-islamic-kingdom-430872.html (29 October, 2010).

sparked protests from some Christians,[24] clearly concerned with a perceived challenge to the established Christian identity of the city. Nevertheless, some Christians did not feel this concern, as is seen in the following media report:

> "Rev Franz Meurer, a Roman Catholic priest in a rough Cologne neighbourhood, led his parish to raise funds for the construction of a controversial mosque there, slated to be Germany's biggest in a city most famous for its Catholic cathedral."[25]

Many other examples exist of grandiose plans to build mosques in various locations in Europe, plans often based on architectural designs that are quite imposing in terms of surrounding landscapes and cityscapes.

Lobby Groups and their Output

Growing communities do not necessarily translate to influence in the corridors of power. For that to happen, there needs to be catalysts for action in the form of groups that engage in lobbying. This can take two forms: one that works within the structures and conventions of the dominant cultures and institutions, and one that is counter-cultural. One of the most interesting and potentially influential examples of the former is the Federation of Islamic Organisations in Europe (FIOE), reportedly inspired by and affiliated with the international Islamist group the Muslim Brotherhood.[26]

Federation of Islamic Organisations in Europe

The FIOE claims to represent 400 Muslim organisations in Europe. Its self-description is a model of Western multicultural-speak: "a

---

[24] http://www.middle-east-online.com/english/?id=27616; http://www.telegraph.co.uk/news/worldnews/1555604/Huge-mosque-stirs-protests-in-Cologne.html

[25] Isabelle de Pommereau "Priest bridges religious divide by funding Germany's biggest mosque", Christian Science Monitor, February 2, 2010.
http://www.csmonitor.com/World/Global-News/2010/0202/Priest-bridges-religious-divide-by-funding-Germany-s-biggest-mosque

[26] Steve Merley, 'The Muslim Brotherhood in Belgium', The NEFA Foundation, May 14, 2008.
http://www.nefafoundation.org/miscellaneous/FeaturedDocs/nefambbelgium0408.pdf (2 November, 2010); 'Muslim Networks and Movements in Western Europe', *Pew Research Centre*, September 15, 2010; http://pewforum.org/Muslim/Muslim-Networks-and-Movements-in-Western-Europe-Muslim-Brotherhood-and-Jamaat-i-Islami.aspx (2 November, 2010).

cultural organization, with hundreds of member organizations spread across 28 European States, all subscribing to a common belief in a methodology based on moderation and balance, which represents the tolerance of Islam."[27]

FIOE has produced the Muslim Charter of Europe, produced by a team who travelled all over Europe taking soundings from Muslim groups on their priorities and concerns. It is worth briefly examining one key article of the Charter.

Article 20 states that "Muslims of Europe are urged to integrate positively in their respective societies, on the basis of a harmonious balance between preservation of Muslim identity and the duties of citizenship. Any form of integration that fails to recognise the right of Muslims to preserve their Islamic personality and the right to perform their religious obligations does not serve the interests of Muslims nor the European societies to which they belong."

This very carefully worded statement seems to affirm integration, but it is a measured integration: one which allows for an ongoing segregation of religious identity for Muslims. This cuts to the very quick of concerns among non-Muslims of lack of integration by Muslim minority communities.

Other Muslim Lobbying

Soft Counter-Cultural Lobbying

Lobbying for Islam does not always present itself in such well-groomed ways as seen with FIOE. Lobbying can be strongly counter-cultural as well, taking the form of non-*cooperation* or, at times, intimidation. One example of localised counter-cultural lobbying is described by David Brown, the head of University Bible Groups, reporting on an incident in a French university:

> "Islamic activists have been active in the university ... They demanded that they should be able to lay out their prayer mats during examinations, for example. Or they refused to take an oral exam with a female professor."[28]

---

[27] http://www.euro-muslim.net/en_about_us.aspx (2 November, 2010).

[28] Agnieszka Tennant, 'The French Reconnection', *Christianity Today*, 9 November 2005, http://www.christianitytoday.com/ct/article_print.html?id=34315 (2 November, 2010).

Echoes of such a separatist mentality were reported in the Belgian French language magazine *Le Vif/L'Express* which carried a five-page spread in its 29 August 2008 issue about Islam in the Belgian school system. It reported on responses to Muslim presence within Belgian schools, providing evidence of a majority non-Muslim accommodation with minority Muslim priorities: halal food is widely offered in Belgian schools, and pork is increasingly banned; Muslim girls are increasingly able to drop gym and swimming classes and not to attend school outings; the requirements of the Ramadan fast were facilitated for Muslim students; prayer facilities were increasingly being provided in schools; and teachers reported feeling that they were being forced to adapt the curriculum in subjects such as geography and history so as not to offend Muslim students, such as decreasing studies of the Holocaust.

Such reports are unlikely to go unchallenged by Muslim advocacy groups. Indeed, Dr Karim Chemlal, head of the League of Muslims in Belgium, accused the exposé in *Le Vif/L'Express* of being shallow and not going into the real debate. Interestingly, Dr Chemlal is also reportedly the President of the Youth and Student Department of FIOE, and has been named as a member of the Islamist group the Muslim Brotherhood in other sources.[29]

Hard Counter-Cultural Lobbying

At times such counter-cultural Muslim "lobbying" has taken a more violent turn. This occurred in France in November 2005, when 6000 vehicles were burnt in riots throughout France by "urban youth", as they were described in the politically correct French Press. More than 1,500 rioters were arrested, and several churches and synagogues were also torched. On 11 November 2005 the French Catholic newspaper *La Croix* published a lengthy article that focused on social disadvantage among immigrant communities,

---

[29] Steve Merley, 'The Muslim Brotherhood in Belgium', The NEFA Foundation, May 14, 2008.
http://www.nefafoundation.org/miscellaneous/FeaturedDocs/nefambbelgium0408.pdf (2 November, 2010); 'Muslim Networks and Movements in Western Europe', *Pew Research Centre*, September 15, 2010. http://pewforum.org/Muslim/Muslim-Networks-and-Movements-in-Western-Europe-Muslim-Brotherhood-and-Jamaat-i-Islami.aspx (2 November, 2010).

making no reference to the fact that the vast majority were Muslim.[30]

Riots also erupted in France in October 2010, ostensibly against government plans to increase the retirement age, but some correspondents saw darker motivations behind the rioters. Ivan Rioufol of the daily *Le Figaro* wrote as follows:

> "the rioters ... are, mainly, from the ghettos. The hooded people aren't marching to defend retirement at 60, or even the welfare system which enticed their parents or grandparents. They're there to battle the Republic, its culture and its most visible symbols: the security forces, the schools. ... these ethnic insurrections of youth who are often of Muslim culture, also reject the state seen as a colonizer and oppressor. These wild people, each time more intrepid and organized, remind us of the failure of their integration."[31]

In a similar vein, German Family Minister Kristina Schroeder criticised Muslim youths for displaying hostility towards Germans. "We are dealing with fundamentally hostile attitudes towards other groups – particularly against Germans and Christians," she said, adding "Such abuse is unfortunately commonplace amongst youths in certain areas – in the school yard, but also in the underground."[32]

Again we find reference to integration, or lack thereof, among immigrant communities, especially Muslims, touching a nerve with European non-Muslims concerned with what they perceive as a segregationist attitude among Muslim minority communities.

---

[30] See my analysis of these riots at 'France is still right about race integration', *The Church Times*, 18 November, 2005, http://www.churchtimes.co.uk/content.asp?id=13716&print=1 (2 November, 2010).

[31] http://islamineurope.blogspot.com/2010/10/france-riots-outbursts-of-hate-and-anti.html#more (26 October, 2010). Original text: "les casseurs ... viennent, majoritairement, des cités-ghettos. Les encapuchonnés ne défilent pas pour défendre la retraite à 60 ans, ni même le système de protection sociale qui a pu attirer leurs parents ou leurs grands-parents. Ils ont là pour en découdre avec la République, sa culture et ses symboles les plus visibles: les forces de l'ordre, les écoles. ... ces insurrections ethniques d'une jeunesse de culture souvent musulmane, le même rejet d'un Etat vu comme colonisateur et oppresseur. Les ensauvagés, chaque fois plus intrépides et organisés, rappellent l'échec de leur intégration." http://blog.lefigaro.fr/rioufol/2010/10/ce-que-revelent-les-intifadas.html (26 October, 2010).

[32] http://www.news24.com/World/News/German-minister-criticises-Muslim-youths-20101102 (3 November, 2010).

Evidence of Integration and/or Reversing Trends?

Is there any evidence of social developments that provide alternative arguments to the view that Muslim minorities do not integrate well?

Some interesting data emerges from research conducted in the Netherlands and Germany. In a 2006 study by the Netherlands Social and Cultural Planning Bureau, the following was reported:

> "The number of kids per Moroccan women has gone down from 6 in 1983 to 3.3 in 2005. Daughters aren't kept home from school and marriage is no longer seen as a reason to stop work. Barely 25% of young women think that women should stay home to care for the children."[33]

It is on the basis of such observations of lower family size among Dutch Muslim immigrants that the Netherlands Interdisciplinary Demographic Institute predicted a Netherlands Muslim minority population of 8% or lower in 2050.[34] This is a far more conservative estimate than that provided by "The Demographic Problem" film, which predicted a 50% Muslim population in the Netherlands within fifteen years.

Across the border in Germany, similar trends in family size were reported in a research monograph in 2009.[35] This research project focused on 5,000 women in West Germany in the years 1984-2004, both Germans and first and second generation immigrants from south and southeastern Europe. Among other findings, the study found that 58.8% of first generation Turkish immigrants have three or more children, but for Turkish second generation immigrants this figure reduces to 34.2% of Turks, pointing to a greater level of integration in terms of family size than is often assumed by critics

---

[33] http://islamineurope.blogspot.com/2006/03/study-of-dutch-immigrant-women.html (2 November, 2010).

[34] http://www.nidi.knaw.nl/en/output/demos/2007/demos-23-09-debeer.pdf/demos-23-09-debeer.pdf (2 November, 2010).

[35] Nadja Milewski, *Fertility of Immigrants: A Two-Generational Approach in Germany* (Demographic Research Monographs, Springer Verlag: Berlin, 2009).

who assert that native Germans will eventually be a minority in the country.[36]

Furthermore, recent immigration statistics for Germany raise questions about some predictions that foresaw a rapid pace of Islamisation of German society. According to German Federal Statistical Office figures for 2009, 721,000 foreigners immigrated to Germany in that year, with the top four source countries being Poland, Romania, the United States and Bulgaria. The fifth ranked source country, Turkey, provided 30,000 of that overall immigration number, but this figure was "roughly equal to the average number of people of Turkish origin who have left Germany annually in recent years."[37] Asylum applications for 2009 included 6,500 people from Iraq, 3,375 from Afghanistan and 1,400 people from Turkey (primarily Kurds).

Returning to the question of the influence of Islamist extremism on European Muslim minorities, while there is cause for concern, the story is not monolithic. This is illustrated in the case of Bosnia Herzegovina. A deadly 2010 attack against a police station in the country pointed to the involvement of the growing radical Islamist Wahhabi movement.[38] Furthermore, there were reports of Wahhabis leafleting mosques throughout Bosnia Herzegovina urging Muslims not to join the country's police and army. Bosnia state security agency OSA director Almir Dzuvo reported some 3,000 well-equipped radical Islamist militants in Bosnia posing a serious terrorism threat to the country.[39] Nevertheless, support for such radical ideologies appeared marginal in the country, with security forces (themselves largely Muslim) being able to draw on

---

[36] http://islamineurope.blogspot.com/2010/08/germany-2nd-generation-immigrants.html (28 October, 2010).

[37] German Federal Statistical Office, 'Searching for Facts in Germany's Integration Debate', Spiegel Online, 12 October, 2010.
http://www.spiegel.de/international/germany/0,1518,druck-722716,00.html (31 October, 2010).

[38] http://news.asiaone.com/News/AsiaOne%2BNews/World/Story/A1Story20100928-239456.html (28 September, 2010).

[39] http://www.adnkronos.com/AKI/English/Security/?id=3.1.835114951 (5 October, 2010).

community support in monitoring and responding to the activities of the radicals.

Muslims Speak through the Polls

In order to assess whether concerns about Muslim attitudes to integration have validity, it is helpful to consider responses to polls taken among European Muslim minority communities.

In 2008 the University of Amsterdam surveyed directly or indirectly 900 young Muslims aged between 15-29 years old. The Muslims surveyed were divided into four groups: Respectful (R - 40%), or those open to the opinions of others; Traditional (T - 40%), or those who highly valued religious laws; Individualizing (I - 13%), or those who did not feel bound by religious laws; and Secular (S - 7%), or those farthest removed from the religious law. The survey revealed a broad range of information, but there were two observations of interest to our discussion.

First, around 59% of respondents said they could definitely be friends with someone who thought completely different about Islam, while around 16.5% disagreed. Around 75% of respondents said they either seldom or sometimes went to mosque, while 25% attended regularly or very often.[40]

Moving to Austria, in 2008 a survey was taken by social scientist Mouhanad Khorchideto to determine the attitudes and beliefs of Austrian Islamic Religious Teachers. His survey reported that 8.5% sympathized with the use of violence to spread Islam; 18.2% supported the death penalty for apostasy; 14.7% opposed the Austrian constitution; 28.4% considered it impossible to be both European and Muslim; and 21.9% opposed democracy.[41] Such figures must be a cause for concern, given the important role played by religious teachers in shaping the attitudes of the Islamic community in Austria. Such figures would of course need to be corroborated from other sources.

---

[40] http://islamineurope.blogspot.com/2008/12/netherlands-study-of-muslim-youth.html (1 November, 2010).

[41] Original source http://gatesofvienna.blogspot.com/; http://hommaforum.org/index.php?topic=1654.0 (1 November, 2010).

Also in Austria, a further survey was commissioned by the Austrian Ministry of the Interior and carried out by Gfk Austria in 2009 to determine the attitudes and beliefs of Austrian Muslims about Sharia Law. More than half of the approximate 220,000 Turkish immigrants were in favour of Islamic law being introduced into the Austrian legal system, according to this survey. It also showed that 72% prioritised the following of religious commandments over democratic requirements. For 57% of the Turks surveyed, the laws and regulations of Islam were more important than those of Austria. And almost half of the Turkish immigrants considered that crime in Austria was caused by democracy. Finally, 76% of Turks surveyed watched Turkish TV almost every day, compared with 30% who watched the Austrian national broadcaster ORF.[42]

In the same year, a study entitled "Your Muslim Neighbor" was conducted among 523 Muslims living in Denmark by Capacent.[43] It showed that 18% of Muslims in Denmark supported the view that "Sharia law should be integrated into Danish law", though 60% don't regularly attend mosques and consider Danish imams unrepresentative.

In the country where the Muhammad cartoon caused such controversy, there was clearly a chasm between Danish non-Muslim and Muslim opinions on questions of freedom of speech. The statement that "It should be forbidden to criticize religion" attracted agreement from 55% of Muslims in Denmark but only 10% of non-Muslim Danes. Furthermore, while 97% of Danish non-Muslims said that terrorism was unacceptable, only 82% of Danish Muslims unequivocally rejected terrorism, with 6% stating that terrorism could be acceptable.

Taking a different angle to the question of attitudes among Muslims in Europe, it is worth taking note of the Gallup Coexist Index 2009, that surveyed Muslims in Germany, France and Britain. It concluded that French Muslims were less conservative in their views, followed by the German and finally the British Muslims.

---

[42] http://islamineurope.blogspot.com/2010/01/austria-majority-of-turks-want-sharia.html (1 November, 2010).

[43] http://islamineurope.blogspot.com/2009/04/denmark-55-of-muslims-think-criticizing.html (1 November, 2010).

For example, none of the 1,001 British Muslims interviewed considered that homosexual acts were morally acceptable. In contrast, the acceptability rate among French Muslims was a surprisingly high 35%. Furthermore, 48% of French Muslims believed sexual relations between unmarried men and women were acceptable, followed by 27% of German Muslims responding favourably. However, only 3% of British Muslims surveyed considered sex outside marriage to be acceptable.

On the thorny issue of integration within broader society, 46 % of French Muslims and 35% of those in Germany regarded themselves as integrated into their society, while the corresponding figure for British Muslims stood at a lowly 10%.

Concluding Remarks

There is undoubtedly widespread public concern across Europe with the growing Islamic minority presence, as is reflected in polls taken of non-Muslims Europeans in various locations. There are two macro reasons for this concern: first, an ongoing problem with international Islamist terrorism directed at the West, and second, a perception that Muslim immigrants to Western countries and their locally born descendents do not integrate to Western norms, but rather seek to redefine society according to Islamic values and priorities.

Political leaders are picking up on these popular concerns and are responding in diametrically opposed ways. Some agree with the concerns and speak out increasingly with stronger statements about the need for Muslim minorities to integrate. Others blame the concerns on irrational Islamophobia, figuratively wagging a scolding finger at European citizens for excluding and alienating Muslim minorities.

The rapid growth of Islamic minority communities, together with hands-off multicultural policies that actively advocated against integration for a generation, have encouraged some Muslim activist groups to not merely preserve their religious and cultural identities but also to seek to redefine majority societies in their own image.

As visible evidence of rapid social change has taken place, it has generated increasing concern on the part of indigenous communities in Europe. This is a concern that is not peculiar to Europeans by any means, but would be shared by any community that sees its world changing rapidly around it and feels itself powerless to act.

The above developments, supplemented by the potent cocktail of increasingly vocal and effective Islamist lobby groups, both "soft" and hard", is creating a pressure-cooker situation in various European locations.

At the same time, Muslim minority communities are by no means monolithic. There is some evidence of integration with successive generations in areas such as family size – in spite of, not because of, official government policies of multiculturalism. Nevertheless, the participation of 2nd and 3rd generation Muslim youth in anti-social activities, including violent rioting, in France suggests that statistically-defined integration does not necessarily lead to social cohesion, and more interventionist policies may be needed to bring this about.

Polls of Muslims show a solid minority core of hard-liners who support terrorism, advocate for Sharia Law in a European context, and build figurative walls of separation between themselves and the majority in European contexts. But the same polls show that there is a body of European Muslims who are potential partners in any campaign to address the widespread concerns and increasing friction between Muslim and non-Muslim Europeans.

Several Recommendations could be made

1) Governments should rein in the speed of social change by turning down (but not off) the tap of immigration, giving priority in immigration policies to those groups which, on evidence, more readily adapt and integrate to the receiving society.

2) Public discourse about immigration should drop "multiculturalism" as the buzz word and replace it with terms such as "social cohesion" and "integration".

3) A two track policy vis-à-vis Muslim communities should be followed, of positive reinforcement of those Muslims who do integrate, and heavy pressure (including deportation) of those engaged in anti-social activities and subversion.

4) The Church should not be quietist in this, staying apart, but should rather be engaged and involved in the challenges facing European societies.

5) Fifth, in speaking into these debates, Christians must speak with both clarity and accuracy, not loosely throwing about wild statistics as is done in the film "The Demographic Problem" but rather presenting information that is solidly researched and is truthful.

A Contrast between Evangelical and Islamic Perspectives towards People with Disabilities with Implications for Evangelical and Muslim Outreach to the Disabled

Ruth Turner

Introduction

> "There are over 500 million people with disabilities in the world today. Of these, 8.5 million – one in seven of the population – live in the U.K."[1]

These statistics may perhaps come as a surprise to many. In the U.K. people with disabilities remain to a certain extent a "hidden", marginalised group. Moreover, Ashif Sindhi, a Muslim who is blind, claims: "Today, although accessibility is gaining higher priority on the agenda in mainstream society barriers are clearly present within various faith-based communities."[2] The focus of this paper is to contrast Evangelical and Muslim perspectives towards people with disabilities with implications for outreach. The aim is to highlight differences between the two perspectives. It is hoped that this would challenge peoples' views towards this 'often forgotten' group.

Before beginning however it is important to consider what is meant by the term "disability."[3]

Models of Disability

The medical model: "According to the British Discrimination Act 1995, a person must have four elements to be considered "disabled":

(1) there must be a physical or mental impairment.

---

[1] Roy McCloughry and Wayne Morris, *Making a World of Difference: Christian Reflections on Disability* (London: SPCK, 2002), 1.

[2] Ashif Sindhi, 'Disability in Islam – Introduction' http://www.wwwl5.redstation.co.uk/masj174242/intro.html (19 October, 2009).

[3] Disability denotes difference. Thomas E. Reynolds, *Vulnerable Communion: A Theology of Disability and Hospitality* (Grand Rapids, Mich.: Brazos Press, 2008), 47.

(2) The impairment must adversely affect the individual's capacity to carry out normal day to day activities.

(3) The adverse affect must be substantial.

(4) The adverse affect must be 'long term'."[4]

The social model: "Processes of disempowerment, exclusion and isolation, concealing deeper attitudinal, employment–related, educational, and architectural obstacles to genuine inclusion ... Thus it is that, as a loss of bodily function, impairment is socially transformed into a disability, a restriction of activity that excludes social participation."[5]

This paper addresses both models – the Evangelical perspective focuses more on the social model while the Muslim perspective predominantly on the medical model. The term "learning disabilities" will be used for mental impairment and "physical disabilities" for physical impairment.

Section 1: An Evangelical Perspective towards People with Disabilities

Introduction

Disability is often "seen as tragic, and thus problematic."[6]

---

[4] Kate Diesfield, 'Disability matters in medical law' *Journal of Medical Ethics* 27 (2001), 388-92. As cited in Vardit Rispler-Chaim, 'Disability in Islamic Law' *International Library of Ethics, Law, and the New Medicine* 32 (The Netherlands: Springer, 2007), 2.

[5] Reynolds, *Vulnerable Communion*, 26.

[6] Frances Young (ed.) *Encounter with Mystery: Reflections on L'Arche and Living with Disability* (London: Darton, Longman and Todd, 1997), ix. "Although the Hebrew Bible has no term that parallels our term "disability" precisely, it does categorise persons on the basis of physical or mental condition, appearance, alleged vulnerability, and the presence or absence of certain diseases, and such classification may result in the text's demand for the exclusion of affected persons from many aspects of social, economic and religious life." Saul M. Olyan, *Disability in the Hebrew Bible: Interpreting Mental and Physical Differences* (Cambridge: Cambridge University Press, 2008), 1. "Perhaps the closest ancient Greek parallel to the modern term "disability" is the word ἀσθενής ("weak") and its correlates." Martin Albl, ' "For Whenever I Am Weak, Then I Am Strong": Disability in Paul's Epistles', in *This Abled Body: Rethinking Disabilities in Biblical Studies* (ed. Hector Avalos, Sarah J. Melcher, and Jeremy Schipper; Semeia Studies 55; Atlanta, Ga.: Society of Biblical Literature, 2007), 146.

This section will consider the Evangelical doctrines of creation, the fall, redemption and consummation with specific reference to people with physical and learning disabilities. Biblical material will be used throughout and there will be a particular focus on the radical example of Christ in the Gospels who crossed social boundaries to minister to the marginalised and the outcast, many of whom had disabilities.[7] Also, as Bowker notes, "in connection with suffering the Gospels are controlled by a knowledge that Jesus met the realities of suffering in his own person and was not defeated by them."[8] The victory he has won is for all people that all may share in it.

Creation

"Let us make man in our image, after our likeness."[9]

All peoples are made in the image of the triune God created for relationship with Him and with one another. So people with disabilities are no less "whole" people than non-disabled people in God's sight – we are all, each one of us "fearfully and wonderfully made"[10] each one with gifts and abilities, and the Lord tells us: "You are precious in my eyes, and honoured, and I love you."[11] While society behaves for the most part "towards the disabled, seeing their disability, not their face,"[12] Jesus reflected the Father's heart in his interaction with this people group. A right perspective towards such people then is to treat them with as much respect and dignity as non-disabled people.

---

[7] McCloughry and Morris, *Making a World of Difference*, 59. cf. Matthew 4: 23-25. Holy Bible, English Standard Version (E.S.V.).

[8] John Bowker, *Problems of Suffering in Religions of the World* (Cambridge: Cambridge University Press, 1970), 46.

[9] Genesis 1: 26.

[10] Psalm 139: 14.

[11] Isaiah 43: 4

[12] David F. Ford, 'L'Arche and Jesus: What is the Theology?' in *Encounter with Mystery: Reflections on L'Arche and Living with Disability* (ed. Frances Young; London: Darton, Longman and Todd, 1997), 81.

The Fall

"Behold, I was brought forth in iniquity, and in sin did my mother conceive me."[13]

Original sin has "radically affected human nature."[14] It is as a direct consequence of Adam's rebellion against God that creation's good and perfect order was disrupted.[15] This is the root cause of why throughout history people have had disabilities, and also why it seems the Lord "creates" individuals with disabilities.[16] "Christians have been particularly exercised by the problem of theodicy – by the difficulty of defending the justice and righteousness of God in face of the existence of evil and suffering."[17] But biblically people have been created with disabilities, or come to have disabilities at some point in their lives, so that they might cry out to the Lord – or that others might do so on their behalf – repent and be saved. It is for God's glory, too, that others might see and believe as well. For according to Moltmann, "A person with disabilities gives others the precious insight into the woundedness and weakness of human life."[18] Frame, too, notes the curse has affected all of humanity in terms of the pain and frustration experienced by each of us: "It is not until we recognise our own disablements that we can reach out to those who are physically disabled."[19]

The incarnate Christ, though, understands human weaknesses. While sinless he identified with different peoples including those

---

[13] Psalm 51: 5.

[14] Bowker, *Problems of Suffering in Religions of the World*, 82.

[15] Cf. Genesis 3.

[16] Psalm 139: 13-16.

[17] Bowker, *Problems of Suffering in Religions of the World*, 81.

[18] Jürgen Moltmann, 'Liberate Yourselves by Accepting One Another', in *Human Disability and the Service of God*, (eds. Nancy L. Eiesland and Don E. Saliers; Nashville: Abingdon, 1998). 105-122, 121. As cited in Reynolds, *Vulnerable Communion*, 210.

[19] John M. Frame, *The Doctrine of the Christian Life: A Theology of Lordship* (Phillipsburg, New Jersey: P&R Publishing, 2008), 683. "In truth, no person is without impairment in some form because none manifests the fullness of the image of God in which we are created." Bruce C. Birch, 'Impairment as a Condition in Biblical Scholarship: A Response', in *This Abled Body: Rethinking Disabilities in Biblical Studies* (ed. Hector Avalos, Sarah J. Melcher, and Jeremy Schipper), 185.

with disabilities.[20] Amanda Shao Tan talks of "the disability of Christ" in terms of "who he became, what he forfeited, and the limitations and confinements to which he subjected himself."[21]

The Mercy of God

"Sin itself is a disability, from which we cannot escape, apart from God's free grace."[22]

a) *The healing of the man born blind*[23]

It is our hearts which are the root of all sin and this is the same for all people.[24] In Jewish tradition a person with physical or learning disabilities was stigmatised socially and their disability was closely associated with individual sin and the demonic.[25] In his Gospel, John recounts Jesus' encounter with a man born blind, "and his disciples asked him, "Rabbi, who sinned, this man or his parents, that he was born blind?""[26] Carson notes here that, "Although Jesus does not disavow the generalizing connection between sin and suffering, he completely disavows a universalizing of *particular* connections."[27] Indeed, "God has a special concern for the disabled."[28] The Old Testament is clear that their abuse is

---

[20] McCloughry and Morris, *Making a World of Difference*, 64.

[21] Amanda Shao Tan, 'The Disabled Christ', *Transformation*, 1998, 15 (4), 12-13. As cited in McCloughry and Morris, *Making a World of Difference*, 65.

[22] Frame, *The Doctrine of the Christian Life*, 683.

[23] Cf. Mark 10: 46-52 and Luke 18: 35-43 – the accounts of the healing of Bartimaeus, another man who was blind. The Greek verb used here when he says to Jesus: "let me recover my sight" (Mark 10: 51b; Luke 18: 41b) is ἀναβλέπω – literally "I look up/ receive sight." This could indicate that Bartimaeus had either been born blind or that he had lost his sight at some later stage in life. *The New Greek-English Interlinear New Testament with the New Revised Standard Version, New Testament* (trans. Robert K. Brown, and Philip W. Comfort; Carol Stream, Ill.: Tyndale House, 1990).

[24] Mark 7: 14-23.

[25] Albl, 'For Whenever I Am Weak, Then I Am Strong',158.

[26] John 9: 2.

[27] D.A. Carson, *The Gospel According to John* (The Pillar New Testament Commentary; Leicester: Apollos, 1991), 362.

[28] Frame, *The Doctrine of the Christian Life*, 683.

prohibited[29] and they also have a prominence in the Lord's redemptive promises.[30]

Jesus alone is able to bring spiritual healing to lives, bringing people from darkness to light – indeed to himself, who is "the light of the world".[31] So first, Jesus healed the man born blind physically[32] although spiritually he "saw" only in part.[33] But later in the account, after the man had been cast out by the Pharisees[34] Jesus *found him*, and revealed his true identity to him.[35] The man believed in him and worshipped him as Lord.[36] Jesus is the one who comes and finds people, reveals himself to them, and gives them his Spirit that they may worship him.[37] No-one is beyond his reach.[38] But "seeing" Jesus spiritually, demands a response. Peoples' sin remains unforgiven unless they turn to him with believing hearts as Lord, as he is the only one who is able to take away their guilt, make them clean, and bring healing to their lives.

b) The Healing of the Paralytic

In the accounts of the paralytic Jesus clearly demonstrates that a person's greatest need is to have their sins forgiven, *not* physical healing.[39] In each of the Synoptic Gospel accounts of this healing, it is on seeing "their faith" – that is the faith of both the paralytic *and* of those who brought him to Jesus – that Jesus' responds. Having claimed to have the authority of God himself, Jesus heals the

---

[29] Frame, *The Doctrine of the Christian Life*, 683. Cf. Leviticus 19: 14.

[30] Frame, *The Doctrine of the Christian Life*, 683. Cf. Isaiah 35: 3-6a.

[31] John 9: 5. Cf. 2 Corinthians 4: 6.

[32] John 9: 6-7.

[33] John 9: 17. Cf. Mark 8: 27-29.

[34] Cf. John 9: 24-34.

[35] John 9: 35-37. Cf. Luke 19: 10; Daniel 7: 13-15.

[36] John 9: 38.

[37] Cf. John 4: 24; Ezekiel 36: 26-27.

[38] Jesus is: "the Saviour of the world." John 4: 42. Cf. John 9: 39-41; Mark 8: 38.

[39] Matthew 9: 1-8; Mark 2: 1-12; Luke 5: 17-26.

paralytic physically and outwardly. This is immediate, and is proof of his inner spiritual healing.[40]

This account also demonstrates that God also looks on the faith of those who care for people with disabilities. Nevertheless, salvation in any circumstance ultimately depends on God's free gift of grace. And, as Abraham says to the Lord in Genesis: "Shall not the Judge of all the earth do what is just?"[41] So, whether a child has disabilities of a profound and multiple nature, and can only communicate through the emotions they display, and are dependent upon total care, or if they are able to communicate and are physically able to care for themselves to a certain extent, and yet do not seemingly have the cognitive ability/ understanding to take that step of faith, still they may be saved.[42]

c) The Banquet Parables

McCloughry and Morris write that Jesus, "reorders the Jewish expectation of what it means for the Kingdom to come by placing poor and disabled people at the heart of the Kingdom; thus showing not only what that Kingdom will be like but something about who God is and what his values are."[43] In healing people Jesus "restores them to community enabling them to work, take care of their families and live in the community."[44]

However in the parables of the banquet in Luke's Gospel[45] not everyone who is invited has "a restored body."[46] In the first parable Jesus teaches his disciples, "to take the initiative to create a diverse community"[47] by inviting people who are different to themselves,

---

[40] Matthew 9: 7-8; Mark 2: 12; Luke 5: 25-26. The right response when this happens in a person's life is to see it as a miracle and to give glory to God.

[41] Genesis 18: 25b.

[42] It could be said that they are like babies/ toddlers in their dependence. Those from Evangelical families, some would claim, would also be saved if they died.

[43] McCloughry and Morris, *Making a World of Difference*, 60.

[44] McCloughry and Morris, *Making a World of Difference*, 60.

[45] Luke 14: 12-24.

[46] McCloughry and Morris, *Making a World of Difference*, 58.

[47] McCloughry and Morris, *Making a World of Difference*, 58.

and cannot repay them,[48] while in the second, "those that come are accepted as they are."[49] Thus, "Jesus shows inclusion is to be a hallmark of the work of his disciples and therefore of the church age."[50]

Faith not Works

It is people's words and actions that are often indicators that they love the Lord. While there are people with disabilities who do have the cognitive ability to be able to communicate their faith, with others it may not be so clear. But Jesus taught that we should all come to him as "little children,"[51] and in this way such people with disabilities can be a real example to non-disabled people. Essentially it is not about what we *do*[52] – we contribute nothing but our sin to our salvation – it is God's work alone[53] and we need to trust that those with disabilities, while they may not be able to communicate in the same way as others, may enjoy a personal relationship with their Lord and Saviour in ways that we may never fully understand; "For all things are possible with God."[54]

Heaven and Hell

Heaven and hell are as real for people with disabilities as they are for non-disabled people. Jesus' priority was sharing the good news of the Kingdom of God with all people,[55] and that should be our priority, too. Jesus' charge in the Gospel accounts both to those he healed and those who witnessed the healings not to tell anyone[56] shows that he did not want to detract from the central focus of his ministry. Not everyone who Jesus healed physically was saved it

---

[48] Cf. Luke 6: 32-34.

[49] McCloughry and Morris, *Making a World of Difference*, 58.

[50] McCloughry and Morris, *Making a World of Difference*, 60.

[51] Cf. Luke 9: 46-48.

[52] Cf. Ephesians 2: 8-9.

[53] Cf. Romans 5: 6-11; Romans 11: 5-6.

[54] Mark 10: 27b.

[55] Mark 1: 14-15.

[56] Cf. Mark 7: 31-37.

seems.[57] Those on the outside will be excluded from God's presence and love for eternity.[58] This is a challenge to reach those with disabilities with the Gospel message.[59] However, we need to communicate the Gospel in a way which is suited to their needs, and here lies the challenge. Nancy Eiseland, who has physical disabilities herself, notes:

> The history of the church's interaction with the disabled is at best an ambiguous one. Rather than being a structure for empowerment, the church has more often supported the societal structures and attitudes that have treated people with disabilities as objects of pity and paternalism. For many disabled persons the church has been a "city on a hill" – physically inaccessible and socially inhospitable.[60]

New Creation

"If anyone is in Christ, he is a new creation. The old has passed away; behold, the new has come."[61]

People with disabilities who belong to Christ have an eternal hope and promise, both now and for the future. Here in this life, they can experience spiritual healing – a restored relationship with the One who knows them intimately, and who loves them unconditionally. Then there is the promise of new bodies in the new creation.[62]

But Eiesland gives this insight into the resurrected Christ, who she describes as, "the disabled God who embodied both impaired hands and feet and pierced side and the *imago Dei*."[63] She continues, "Paradoxically, in the very act commonly understood as the transcendence of physical life, God is revealed as tangible, bearing

---

[57] Cf. Luke 17: 11-19.

[58] Matthew 13: 49-50.

[59] Cf. "The Great Commission" - Matthew 28: 18-20; Mark 1: 17.

[60] Nancy L. Eiesland, *The Disabled God: Toward a Liberatory Theology of Disability* (Nashville, Tenn.: Abingdon Press, 1994), 20.

[61] 2 Corinthians 5: 17.

[62] Cf. 1 Corinthians: 15: 35-57; Luke 24: 36-39; Philippians 3: 20-21; Revelation 21: 4-5a.

[63] Eiesland, *The Disabled God,* 99.

the representation of the body reshaped by injustice and sin into fullness of the Godhead."[64]

Conclusion

All people, whether disabled or non-disabled, are helpless without God's intervention in terms of their salvation. Just as God has had mercy on us, so Jesus taught us to show compassion and mercy to those who are vulnerable and have significant needs[65] – those who are so often marginalised in our society, and even our churches.[66] Jesus' interaction with the disabled should be a model for our own interaction as we seek as Christians to be conformed to the image of Christ.[67]

Section 2: An Islamic Perspective towards People with Disabilities

Introduction

In this section we will consider the Islamic doctrines of creation, sin and suffering, and salvation in the light of people with disabilities and with reference to the Qur'an and Islamic *shari'a*. The views of a Sunni Muslim and a Shi'ite Muslim will form an integral part of this section.

Creation

"Naught is as His likeness; and He is the Hearer, the Seer."[68] Allah is the Creator God according to the Qur'an.[69] Islam teaches that

---

[64] Eiesland, *The Disabled God*, 99-100. Morris comments, "the arguments about God as disabled, stem from searching for a way of finding God being able to identify with the experience of the disabled person today." Wayne Morris, *Theology without Words: Theology in the Deaf Community* (Explorations in Practical, Pastoral and Empirical Theology; Hampshire: Ashgate, 2008), 146.

[65] Cf. "The Good Samaritan" - Luke 10: 25-37.

[66] Cf. James 1: 22-25.

[67] Cf. Romans 8: 29.

[68] Sura 42, 11. *The Meaning of the Glorious Qur'an* (trans. Mohammed Marmaduke Pickthall; New Delhi, India: Idara Isha'at-E-Diniyat (P) Ltd., 1994). But the Qur'an also teaches that Allah is nearer to man "than his jugular vein." 50, 16.

[69] "We have created you from dust, then from a drop of seed, then from a clot, then from a little lump of flesh shapely and shapeless." 22, 5. Cf. 23, 12-14.

Allah has a special regard for humankind: "Verily We have honoured the children of Adam. We carry them on the land and the sea, and have made provision of good things for them, and have preferred them above many of those whom We created with a marked preferment."[70]

However, sura 22.5 speaks of untimely death and dementia: "And among you there is he who dieth (young), and among you there is he who is brought back to the most abject time of life, so that, after knowledge, he knoweth naught." So how does Islam account for this, and more specifically for people having disabilities?[71] For in Islam there is no doctrine of the Fall – Adam's sin is not seen to have any repercussions for his descendants since the Qur'an says that he repented and Allah "accepted his repentance."[72]

The Question of Suffering[73]

According to the Qur'an, suffering "is within the control of God, and that in a sense, therefore, it comes from him."[74] The Sunni Muslim writes,

> Islam has a very strongly predestinarian tradition which upholds the sovereignty of God in divinely ordering creation and human lives according to His Will. There is ample material in the Quran which supports the view that things are as they are because it is "written" this way by God, and this forms a constant refrain throughout Islam's sacred scripture. Islam asserts itself to be *dīn alfira* ("the religion of the

---

[70] 17, 70. Cf. 95, 4.

[71] Ghaly writes regarding measures: "within the realm of "physical" treatment ... believed to prevent the occurrence of disability." He says: "Discouraging consanguineous marriage by the majority of jurists is (a) clear step in this regard. However, other jurists in the early and modern times still object to this discouragement and insist there is no harm in conducting this type of marriage." Mohammed M. Ghaly, 'Physical and Spiritual Treatment of Disability in Islam: Perspectives of Early and Modern Jurists', *Journal of Religion, Disability and Health* 12 Part 2 (2008), 134. According to the Qur'an specific family-members cannot marry each other (4, 23) but first cousin marriage is permissible (33, 50). As cited in Ghaly, "Physical and Spiritual Treatment of Disability in Islam," 113-114.

[72] Moucarry, *Faith to Faith*, 95. Cf. 2, 36-37. The Qur'an teaches that man is born morally pure. Sin, it says, is disobeying the will of Allah.

[73] 64, 11: "No calamity befalleth save by Allah's leave."

[74] Bowker, *Problems of Suffering in Religions of the World*, 105.

natural order"), and central to its belief is that all things are as they are because God has in His Wisdom decreed that it should so be."[75]

The Shi'ite adds: "We are not able to challenge our God – we are creations."[76]

But why would Allah bring about suffering? A Muslim understanding as to why this happens (and we may assume that those with disabilities fall into this category) may be for one of two reasons: as punishment for sin,[77] or as a trial or test.[78] Unbelievers fall into the first category, while Muslims fall into the second.[79]

Suffering will come as a way of testing faith, that those with disabilities might remain loyal and devout to Allah. The appropriate response to disabilities should be one of acceptance or *sabr* – patience and endurance.[80] According to the Shi'ite Muslim, "based on Islamic religion we can't say a person is not 'good' or deformed because we should be thankful for the condition of life God has given you – it is the best situation. If something is missing from you ... one is not able to complain and say God does not like me – this is inappropriate."[81] The Qur'an also teaches that even where suffering

---

[75] Personal communication. 16 October, 2009.

[76] Personal communication. 2 October, 2009. He continued, "We could raise similar questions: why is this one beautiful and this one not?"

[77] Bowker, *Problems of Suffering in Religions of the World*, 106. However, man's sins cannot offend Allah since He is transcendent: "Our disobedient acts do not fundamentally alter our status: although disobedient, we remain God's servants and are able to compensate for our bad deeds by doing good works." Moucarry, *Faith to Faith*, 99. Cf. 65, 1; 6, 160; 16, 61; 6, 134.

[78] Bowker, *Problems of Suffering in Religions of the World*, 109. Cf. 21, 35.

[79] "If ye have received a blow, the (disbelieving) people have received a blow the like thereof. These are (only) the vicissitudes which We cause to follow one another for mankind, to the end that Allah may know those who believe and may choose witnesses from among you; and Allah loveth not wrong-doers. And that Allah may prove those who believe, and may blight the disbelievers. Or deemed ye that ye would enter Paradise while yet Allah knoweth not those of you who really strive, nor knoweth those (of you) who are steadfast?" Sura 3, 140-142.

[80] Bowker, *Problems of Suffering in Religions of the World*, 114. "This, then, becomes a fundamental part of the attitude of Islam, of right relationship with God, submission." Bowker, *Problems of Suffering in Religions of the World*, 105.

[81] Personal communication.

is a form of punishment, if endured faithfully this will be counted towards the final acquittal of an individual's sins.[82]

Moreover, it says that society should respond to those who suffer – and we may assume that this would include those with disabilities – in a way that reflects Allah's character, his justice and compassion.[83] The Sunni says, "there is a clear belief that creation is so ordered by God's Will to emphasise our diversity and that we may come to understand and know one another. The creation of people in variety of gender, ethnicity, intellect and physical abilities limitations, is thus the natural part of God's plan."[84]

Faith and Obedience

The Qur'an teaches that, "people, though sinners, can present themselves before a merciful God with their own moral record and thus be hopeful of their salvation."[85] In Islam both faith and works are requirements for salvation.[86] This means an individual must affirm the 'articles of faith' – belief in one God, his angels, his Prophets, his Books and a Day of Judgement – and also fulfill certain obligations, the most prominent of which are the religious duties or the five 'pillars of Islam.' These are the Shahada (reciting 'the confession of faith'),[87] salat (ritual prayer), zakat (statutory almsgiving), sawn (annual fasting), and hajj (pilgrimage to Mecca).

But what does Allah require of someone who has disabilities? What happens if a person cannot articulate their faith or physically perform these obligations?

First, those with learning disabilities are regarded "like children" in Islam.[88] The Sunni Muslim writes, "People who lack reason by

---

[82] Bowker, *Problems of Suffering in Religions of the World*, 112.

[83] Bowker, *Problems of Suffering in Religions of the World*, 117. Cf. 38, 26.

[84] Personal communication.

[85] Moucarry, *Faith to Faith*, 110.

[86] Cf. 4, 13-14; 9, 4.

[87] 'I bear witness that there is no god but God, and that Muhammad is the Prophet of God.'

[88] The Sunni Muslim writes of those: "who lack mental capacity being regarded as *bāri* ("innocent") and thus like children, automatically sinless and saved." Personal communication.

virtue of their suffering from a mental illness, or who are insane are considered in Islamic theology to be innocent, and like minors and infants are automatically saved in the Hereafter."[89] As such they are not expected to observe any of the obligations incumbent upon Muslims.[90] Rispler-Chaim adds, "This means that as long as their disability persists, even if they have performed a duty they will win no religious merit for it."[91]

But does this include all people with learning disabilities, since this encompasses such a wide range of different people? According to the Shi'ite Muslim, "they are not responsible for Islamic requirements because they don't even understand the meaning of responsibility. It doesn't matter where they are on the spectrum. They are exempt."[92]

Those with physical disabilities, though, are not necessarily exempt from these obligations (depending on their degree of disability), and are prescribed alternative ways of fulfilling them according to their needs. These are detailed in Islamic *shari'a*. Since the Qur'an states that Allah desires the ease not hardship of believers,[93] the Sunni notes, "The manner in which Islamic theology articulates with the praxis of the believer in the real world is substantially through this religious law, and scholars argue in great depth as to what

---

[89] Personal communication. Neither those with learning difficulties or children are considered legally responsible for their deeds. Vardit Rispler-Chaim, *Disability in Islamic Law* (International Library of Ethics, Law, and the New Medicine 32; The Netherlands: Springer, 2007), 38.

[90] "The insane (majnun), the epileptic (masru'), the mentally deficient (ma'tuh) and the unconscious (maghmiyy 'alayhi) are not liable for the performance of any religious duty." Rispler-Chaim, *Disability in Islamic Law*, 20. Cf. 9, 91.

[91] Rispler-Chaim, *Disability in Islamic Law*, 20. "Only the Hanafis diverge on this issue and explain that the *ma 'tuh*, being a harmless person who lacks reason, whose speech is confused, and whose actions are wrong, indeed does not have to perform *wudu'*. But if he has performed *wadu'* the duty fulfilled following it is considered valid." 'Abd al-Rahman Al-Jaziri, *Kitab al-Fiqh 'ala al-Madhahib al-Arba 'a* (Cairo: Dar al-Irshad lilTiba'a wal-Nashr, 1990; Beruit: Dar al-Thaqalayn, 1998), v. 1, 119. As cited in Rispler-Chaim, *Disability in Islamic Law*, 20.

[92] Personal communication.

[93] Cf. 23, 78; 64, 16.

concessions are to be made for people with disabilities as a mercy and a kindness."[94]

These religious duties will now be considered in more detail.

a) Ritual Ablutions

"The major prerequisite for the validity of most of the religious engagements is that the believer maintains a state of purity and cleanliness, *tahara*."[95] Purity is achieved by acts of self-purification, generally with water,[96] which precede rituals like prayer.[97]

> *Wudu'* involves washing one's hands to the elbows, one's face, and one's feet to above the ankles, and wiping one's head with wet hands. It has to be performed with the proper intention (*niya*). Once performed, there are certain elements that may violate the state of purity. These elements are urine, faeces, bad odour emanating from the rectum or urinary tract, and blood. More violations to the state of purity are anything that comes out of the body, such as pus from abscesses and bleeding from wounds.[98]

So what happens when someone with a disability suffers from urine incontinence, for example? Solutions following legal discussions include, "to pray as it is," or alternatively after each prayer to repeat the ablution,[99] or following one *wadu'*, to combine prayers.[100]

---

[94] Personal communication. 23, 62: "And We task not any soul beyond its scope, and with Us is a Record which speaketh the truth, and they will not be wronged." Cf. 2, 286.

[95] Rispler-Chaim, *Disability in Islamic Law*, 19.

[96] wudu' (partial ablution); ghusl (washing of the whole body); tayammum (purifying oneself with sand instead of water). Rispler-Chaim, *Disability in Islamic Law*, 19. Cf. 5, 6.

[97] An individual can have help to do this. Thelma Sangster and Sister Gulshan Esther, *The Torn Veil* (Fort Washington, Pa.: CLC, 2004), 8.

[98] Al-Jaziri, *Kitab al-Fiqh 'ala al-Madhahib al-Arba 'a*, v. 1, 164. As cited in Rispler-Chaim, *Disability in Islamic Law*, 20.

[99] Jamal al-Din Miqdad b. 'Abd Allah Al-Suyuri Al-Hilli (d. 826H/1422), *Al-Tanqih al-Ra'i 'liMukhtasar al-Shara'i'* (Qom: Matba'at al-Khiyam, 1983), v. 1, 87. As cited in Rispler-Chaim, *Disability in Islamic Law*, 21.

[100] Ayatollah Hasan Al-Ha'iri, *Ahkam al-Shi'a* (Kuwait: Maktabat al-Imam Ja'far al-Sadiq 'alayhi al-salam, 1972), v. 1-3, 83. As cited in Rispler-Chaim, *Disability in Islamic Law*, 21.

b) Prayer[101]

"Such as remember Allah, standing, sitting and reclining, and consider the creation of the heavens and the earth."[102]

Other postures are considered valid when praying. However, prayers must still be performed in the direction of Mecca, and at the prescribed times.[103] But the prayers of the blind and the sick are still valid if they are not facing in the right direction.[104] Also if someone is unable to move due to sickness, they are required to "pray with their hearts."[105] The Shi'ite Muslim adds, "Even someone who cannot speak must still pray in his heart."[106]

c) Almsgiving[107]

"Establish worship, and pay the poor-due; and whatever of good ye send before (you) for your souls, ye will find it with Allah."[108]

While people with learning disabilities are not held accountable for paying *zakat*,[109] "if the assets, not the owner, are subject to taxation, the disability or legal incapacity of the owner is disregarded."[110] Those that are financially poor because they are disabled, however, may be allocated *zakat* resources.[111]

---

[101] Cf. 4, 103; 30, 17; 23, 9-11. It is necessary to make up for missed prayers (*qada'*). Qutb al-Din Sa'id b. Hibat Allah Al-Rawandi (d.573H/1178), *Fiqh al-Qur'an* (Qom: Al-Matba'a al-'Ilmiyya, 1976), v. 1, 123. As cited in Rispler-Chaim, *Disability in Islamic Law*, 24.

[102] 3, 191. The ritual prostrate prayer of a believer is a sign of humility. Muslims believe that it is Muhammad who intercedes on their behalf.

[103] 'Abd Allah b. Yusef Al-Juwayni (d. 438H/1046), *Al-Tabsira* (Beruit: Dar al-Kutub al-'Ilmiyya, 1994), 105. As cited in Rispler-Chaim, *Disability in Islamic Law*, 25.

[104] Rispler-Chaim, *Disability in Islamic Law*, 25.

[105] Rispler-Chaim, *Disability in Islamic Law*, 25.

[106] Personal communication.

[107] Cf. 2, 43; 23, 78; 24, 56; 73, 20. Almsgiving is often linked with prayer in the Qur'an.

[108] 2, 110.

[109] Rispler-Chaim, *Disability in Islamic Law*, 38.

[110] Rispler-Chaim, *Disability in Islamic Law*, 38.

[111] Rispler-Chaim, *Disability in Islamic Law*, 38-39.

d) Fasting[112]

"(Fast) a certain number of days; and (for) him who is sick among you, or on a journey, (the same) number of other days; and for those who can afford it there is a ransom: the feeding of a man in need – But whoso doeth good of his own accord, it is better for him: and that ye fast is better for you if ye did but know."[113]

Ramadan is a *fard'ayn* – each person "owes the fast to Allah."[114] But the Shi'ite Muslim says, "Fasting for ill people is not possible. If they fast they will sin."[115] So, if someone's disability prevents them from fasting (for example, advice for paralyzed people is not to fast)[116] alternatives entitle the individual "to merit similar to that of the actual fast."[117] This includes: "feeding the poor for each day of fasting that was missed, or giving charity of the same value."[118] The principle is the lost days are redeemed through "charity."[119]

e) Pilgrimage[120]

"And pilgrimage to the House is a duty unto Allah for mankind, for him who can find a way thither."[121]

The journey and rituals of the *hajj* are physically very demanding.[122] However, "the general attitude seems to be that as long as the pilgrim is conscious and aware of the import of the rituals and

---

[112] Cf. 2, 183, 185, 187. Ramadan lasts for 1 month.

[113] 2, 184.

[114] Rispler-Chaim, *Disability in Islamic Law*, 27.

[115] Personal communication.

[116] Rispler-Chaim, *Disability in Islamic Law*, 33.

[117] Rispler-Chaim, *Disability in Islamic Law*, 32.

[118] Rispler-Chaim, *Disability in Islamic Law*, 28.

[119] Rispler-Chaim, *Disability in Islamic Law*, 28.

[120] Cf. 2, 196; 22, 26 ff.

[121] 3, 97. Wherein are plain memorials (of Allah's guidance); the place where Abraham stood up to pray; and whosoever entereth it is safe. 3, 97.

[122] Rispler-Chaim, *Disability in Islamic Law*, 34.

holiness of time and place (*'aqil*), he or she can successfully complete the duty of the *hajj*. Being in need of one sort of assistance or another does not diminish the religious merit earned."[123] According to the Shi'ite Muslim, "those who have disabilities must still complete the *hajj* by being carried."[124] But if a disabled person is not able to do the *hajj*, they may pay someone to do it on their behalf.[125] The religious authorities (*muftis*) "are invoked to legitimize the *hajj* of the disabled person when it differs from the normal performance due to medical causes."[126]

The Day of Judgement

Salvation in Islam is eschatological, and ultimately dependent upon Allah's sovereignty.[127] So someone who is physically disabled may have lived their life according to the teaching of Islam, including performing all the religious observances, and yet they would not have done any more than carrying out their duty to Allah.[128]

The Qur'an teaches that when a person sins, he disobeys Allah's commands and this has consequences for the individual.[129] As such he needs to seek divine forgiveness.[130] But ultimately good deeds

---

[123] Rispler-Chaim, *Disability in Islamic Law*, 36. So, for example, people who are blind could successfully complete it. Rispler-Chaim, Disability *in Islamic Law*, 37.

[124] Personal communication.

[125] Rispler-Chaim, *Disability in Islamic Law*, 35. "If a financially able person dies before accomplishing the duty of the hajj, either in person or through a hired substitute, the heirs will have to pay for a substitute to accomplish a hajj from the deceased's inheritance, as they must do with regard to other debts of the deceased." Abu Ishaq Al-Shirazi (d. 476H/1083), *Al-Muhadhdhab fi Fiqh al-Imam al-Shafti'i*. (Damascus: Dar al-Qalam, Beruit: Al-Dar al-Shamiyya, 1992), v. 2, 673.

[126] Rispler-Chaim, *Disability in Islamic Law*, 34-35, 37. Generally to be able to do the pilgrimage the conditions require that a person can walk or ride an animal.

[127] Moucarry, *Faith to Faith*, 101, 104. It is also dependent on Muhammad's intercession on the Day of Judgement.

[128] Moucarry, *Faith to Faith*, 104. Obedience though does contribute significantly to a Muslim's salvation. Moucarry, *Faith to Faith*, 102.

[129] Moucarry, *Faith to Faith*, 95. "And whoso transgresseth Allah's limits, he verily wrongeth his soul." 65, 1.

[130] Moucarry, *Faith to Faith*, 103. Cf. 4, 99.

will outweigh evil deeds.[131] The Qur'an speaks of a Day of Judgement where there will be scales on which people's deeds will be weighed – "those whose scales are heavy" will go to Paradise where they will live and experience pleasures for evermore.[132] However, for "those whose scales are light" – the wicked and unbeliever – hell is the place where they will be consumed by fire and torment.[133]

Paradise

The Qur'an talks of future physical resurrection[134] and the hope of Paradise for believers – or at least for those who have done good works. However, what will those with disabilities be like in Paradise?

The Shi'ite points to the Qur'an and says, "Someone who is blind would be blind and missed the way in the other world. Some say this means if someone is blind they will be blind in Paradise. Others see this as a metaphor for spiritual blindness."[135] His personal belief is that we will all be equal – that there will be new bodies/ minds in Paradise.[136] However, the Sunni writes, "Good question! Not sure I know the answer, nor have I been able to find in the Scripture or commentaries any indication of whether people who die disabled or in old age live in Paradise at their elderly age of death, or in the bloom of youth. I would be fascinated to hear if Christian theologians have any view on this."[137]

Conclusion

It seems that those with disabilities can be divided into two groups according to Islamic teaching. Those with learning disabilities have a greater certainty of salvation. As the Shi'ite says, this "is based on

---

[131] 11, 114; 6, 160.

[132] 23, 102. Cf. 2, 25.

[133] 23, 103-104. Cf. 9, 68.

[134] Al-Qiyâmah: Surah 75. Cf. 17, 49; 23, 16; 28, 61; 56, 47-50.

[135] Personal communication.

[136] Personal communication.

[137] Personal communication.

the sovereignty and choice of God. In this case probably they will be in eternity because he hasn't asked of them any duty and therefore they haven't missed any duties unlike able-bodied Muslims."[138] But, for many with physical disabilities life would have to be lived in a way where they fulfilled their duties to Allah to the best of their ability. They would have to trust in Allah's kindness on the Day of Reckoning, for as the Shi'ite comments: "Duties may be changed and converted and modified but still must be done."[139]

The Contrast between Evangelical/ Muslim Perspectives

Table 1: A summary of different perspectives towards people with disabilities

Doctrine	Evangelicals	Muslims
Creation	People with disabilities are made in God's image.	Allah is transcendent and completely "other", but not distant from humankind.[140]
Sin and Suffering	Disabilities are a direct consequence of the Fall.[141]	<ul><li>Muslims have disabilities as a test of faith from Allah</li><li>Unbelievers have disabilities as a punishment for sin</li></ul>

---

[138] Personal communication.

[139] Personal communication.

[140] Moucarry, *Faith to Faith*, 87.

[141] In the Psalms David asks God to afflict his enemies. This could be seen as David asking God to 'disable' his enemies because of their sin. Louise Prideaux, personal communication, 29 December, 2009.

Salvation	It is by grace *alone* that people with disabilities are saved. God will judge in righteousness. Those who love Jesus have a restored relationship with God in this life.	Salvation is based on works *alone*,[142] but people with learning disabilities are not deemed capable of fulfilling Islamic *shari'a* with "full awareness and true intent,"[143] and are therefore exempt from duties. They have more of a 'certainty' of salvation that people with physical disabilities, who are still required to perform certain obligations, do not have.
Resurrection	In the life to come those saved have the assurance of new resurrection bodies.	There is nothing in Islamic Scripture to indicate what resurrection bodies will be like.

Having summarized the main differences between the two perspectives, the implications for Evangelical and Muslim outreach will now be considered.

Section 3: Evangelical and Muslim Outreach to the Disabled

The previous sections outlined the theological differences between Evangelical and Muslim perspectives towards people with disabilities. This section now highlights how this different theology is shown in practice, focusing on two outreaches – one Evangelical and one Muslim.[144]

Evangelical Outreach

This section will focus on an outreach run by Haywards Heath Evangelical Free Church in Sussex. It also draws on the experience of one of its leaders, Simon Howard, who has been involved with the outreach from its outset.[145] The church runs a Causeway group

---

[142] Although certain people groups are exempt.

[143] Rispler-Chaim, Disability in Islamic Law, 26.

[144] There are many organisations in the U.K. that work with people with disabilities. See Appendix 1 for some examples.

[145] The church has run their Causeway group since 1990. Simon Howard, personal communication, 12 December, 2009.

facilitated by the national organization, Causeway Prospects, which seeks to reach those with learning disabilities for Christ.

a) Creation

Causeway, as an Evangelical group, seeks to reach people with a learning disability since their belief is that they reflect God's image as much as anyone else.[146] People with a range of disabilities form the group – some only need minimal support, while others need full-time care. Some have physical disabilities too. Simon observes that, "Their range of personalities is no different to others and each in their own way engage with the meetings."[147] As Christ showed compassion and concern for individuals particularly those who were marginalised, so "building friendships is an important aspect of the work."[148] He comments that working with such people is humbling – that they are "a constant reminder of the importance of 'who we are' rather than our achievements and possessions."[149]

b) Sin

Simon affirms the Evangelical belief of the universal nature of sin: "As an overall working principle we believe that people with a learning disability still need to repent and believe as others and that God knows who are his own."[150]

c) Salvation

Causeway's main principles are based on the Evangelical understanding that the Gospel is good news for everyone:

---

[146] "In the UK one in fifty people have a learning difficulty." Causeway Statement. See Appendix 2.

[147] Howard, personal communication.

[148] Howard, personal communication. After the meetings there are "refreshments and a time for personal conversations." Causeway Statement. Simon explains: "Some are better able to express themselves verbally whilst others express themselves simply through a desire to attend Causeway and church meetings."

[149] Howard, personal communication. In terms of the church as a whole he has seen that the presence of people with disabilities "can help a church to 'get used to' people who are 'different' and therefore become more welcoming and accepting of a wider range of people from society."

[150] Howard, personal communication.

"All people should have an opportunity to hear the Christian message including those with a learning difficulty."[151]

"All people are capable of responding to the Christian message because it is a matter of belief and trust, not intellect and ability."[152]

Twenty to thirty people attend the meetings held once a month, including the team.[153] Meetings are evangelistic in style, "on the principle that often only God will know who is responding in faith."[154] The first hour focuses on singing, Bible teaching, sharing and praying.[155] The team seek to give the group opportunities "to respond to God,"[156] using songs with repetition, percussion instruments, and drama for storytelling. In this way the Gospel is made accessible to all the group members and they are able to join in worship in a way that is appropriate for them.

God has clearly blessed the work of the group over the years. Group members have grown in their awareness of the Lord and some have come to a saving faith.[157]

d) Resurrection

For the team, as Evangelical believers, the joy of seeing people find, "personal fulfilment through believing and trusting in Jesus

---

[151] Causeway Statement.

[152] Causeway Statement.

[153] Causeway Statement. There are eleven in the team, both leaders and helpers, plus two additional associate helpers. They provide the musical accompaniment. Simon Howard writes, "We place a strong emphasis on team work that involves planning and praying together as well as combining our different skills and aptitudes. Bible teaching is at the centre of our Causeway meetings and three of us share this task." Howard, personal communication.

[154] Howard, personal communication.

[155] Causeway Statement.

[156] Causeway Statement.

[157] Causeway Statement. Some of the Causeway group attend the main church services. Three of them have become church members all of whom demonstrate a clear faith. They are integrated into "the full life of the church" as much as is possible. Howard, personal communication.

Christ,"[158] means the assurance, too, that they will have an eternal hope of a restored body and mind.

Muslim Outreach

This section focuses on one Muslim's experience of seeking to help people with disabilities. Ahmad Nazir[159] lives and works in a large English city. Three years ago he was asked if he would be interested in doing something for Muslims with disabilities linked to the mosque he has attended for a number of years.

a) Creation

Ahmad affirms the Islamic belief that a disabled person has a few more obstacles/ tests to get on with life, but also claims that a disabled person is more blessed than a non-disabled person, and is closer to Allah.[160] Ahmad himself lost his sight completely ten years ago.[161]

b) Suffering

Since suffering is regarded as a test from Allah, Ahmad notes, "Within the Muslim community, people with disabilities tend to remain isolated. Families caring for people with severe disabilities receive very little support from their religious communities. Muslims with disabilities also feel excluded from learning and engaging in spiritual and social activities."[162] He aims to "provide information, help and advice for disabled people within an Islamic context."[163] He works on a voluntary basis,[164] but sees his as a

---

[158] Causeway Statement.

[159] His real name has been withheld to maintain confidentiality.

[160] Personal communication.

[161] His "vision" is to try and make people more aware of disabilities. Personal communication.

[162] Ahmad believes that both the able and disabled should have equal access to Islam.

[163] He has written a section on the mosque's website "Disability in Islam" which includes an audio broadcast. A week or two into launching the site he heard people talking about it in the mosque as he walked in. He sees it as "a turning point" and says that people are "starting to take notice." Personal communication.

necessary service since, "trying to find the right advice is difficult" for those with disabilities. With regards to places who say they cater for people with disabilities, he says this is often "just a tick in a box – whether they do it in real life situations is a totally different thing."[165] Often he will pass questions and queries he receives on to others who are better qualified to help.[166] So Ahmad deals with the "practical elements" that people with disabilities may have. He argues that preserving "their rights, humanity, and dignity,"[167] reflects a basic Islamic duty – "to have mercy on others." But any *'why?'* type question he says he would always refer to the imam who is best qualified to answer such questions.

c) Salvation

In Islam, salvation is based on fulfilling obligations, and Ahmad writes of a vision, "that includes full access for people with disabilities by promoting principles of accessibility."[168] The mosque itself is a large, purpose built, and well-furnished mosque, accessible for people with physical disabilities.[169] In Islam, "Public prayer is on

---

[164] He mainly corresponds with people by email and phone from his home. He receives enquiries from Muslims throughout the U.K., from Bedford to Scotland. Personal communication.

[165] Personal communication.

[166] This may include advice about the benefit system, for example.

[167] Dr. Musa al-Basit, *The Rights of the Physically and Mentally Challenged in the Islamic Shari'a* (Um El-Fahem: The Center for Contemporary Studies, 2000). As cited in Rispler-Chaim, *Disability in Islamic Law*, 129.

[168] Ahmad Nazir, 'Disability in Islam – Our Vision', n.p.

[169] There is a lift to the upper floor where the main prayer room is. This has chairs around the outside for those who need a seat. There are rooms downstairs too where people with physical disabilities could pray in a smaller/ more private space. "Two or more persons constitute a jama'a (group of praying people). In any jama'a one person should always step forward and lead the rest in prayer. For Friday prayer, the size of the group which is necessary to render the public prayer valid differs among the various schools of law." Rispler-Chaim, *Disability in Islamic Law*, 25. There is also a sound system which has a "loop" facility and through which prayers/ sermons can be transmitted to all parts of the mosque. This would facilitate Muslims who were deaf/ hard of hearing. While there are no disabled-access toilets, apart from the squat toilets, there are two western-style toilets. For any Muslims with disabilities who come to the mosque to pray apparently it is acceptable for them to perform their ritual ablutions by bathing or showering at home beforehand.

the whole more meritorious than an individual's prayer."[170] Nevertheless, it seems that he is currently the only Muslim with a disability who attends public Friday prayer.[171] This situation seems to reflect Islamic legal attitudes to Muslims who are disabled with regards to the performance of religious duties since they are often given exemptions.[172]

d) Resurrection

For Muslims who are "sane" the hope of Paradise is dependent on the mercy of Allah. But Ahmad comments that it is important to cater for every disability at the mosque, and says that people with learning disabilities perform prayers there too. This is surprising since it seems generally accepted in Islamic theology that this group of people are exempt from such duties, yet will be in Paradise.

Outreach Summary

The approaches of these two outreaches are very different. The work of Causeway is primarily to proclaim the Gospel to those with learning disabilities. The outreach at the mosque focuses on supporting and catering for the needs of Muslims with disabilities. While both types of outreach are valid, the driving force behind each outreach needs to be considered.

The Evangelical approach is based on the Great Commission that Christ gave his followers to go and make disciples. The belief is that a disabled person's greatest need is spiritual healing, for God looks on a person's heart not on their outward appearances.

---

[170] Abu 'AbdAllah Muhammad b. Ahmad al-Ansari Al-Qurtubi (671H/1272), *Al-Jami'liAhkam al-Qur'an* (Beruit: Dar al-Fikr, 1993, v. 1), 326-9. As cited in Rispler-Chaim, *Disability in Islamic Law*, 25.

[171] At prayer times he follows what is happening from what is being said, but says it can be difficult if he comes in late to know whether people are sitting down or standing up. But genuine mistakes are accepted and there is a lot of tolerance. Personal communication.

[172] Duties are lessened for people with disabilities. Dr Musa al-Basit, *The Rights of the Physically and Mentally Challenged in the Islamic Shari'a*. As cited in Rispler-Chaim, *Disability in Islamic Law*, 126. "The public Friday prayer, according to Shi'i jurists, is required of anyone who fulfills the following criteria: he is male, mature, sane, free, healthy, not blind, not lame, not an old man who hardly moves about, and not a traveller; and the distance from his residence to the Friday mosque does not exceed two farsakh (1 farsakh equals three miles)." Al-Rawandi, Fiqh al-Qur'an, v. 1, 133. As cited in Rispler-Chaim, *Disability in Islamic Law*, 24.

The Muslim approach is based on fulfilling duties to Allah – religious duties, and duties of moral care for others. "Islam is a law-based religion,"[173] and this is reflected in its practice. Duties must be performed in order to attain salvation, though there are exceptions for Muslims with disabilities.

Conclusion

The aim of this paper has been to show the contrast between Evangelical and Muslim perspectives towards people with disabilities.

As has been outlined, the Evangelical perspective involves recognising that people have disabilities as a result of the Fall, yet are made in God's image and for his glory. Salvation is based on his grace alone and those that are his have the promise of restored bodies for eternity.

The Islamic perspective recognises Allah as transcendent yet not absent from humankind/ his creation.[174] Unbelievers with disabilities have them as punishment for sin. Muslims with disabilities are being tested in their faith by Allah. Those with physical disabilities who remain faithful and fulfil their duties have the hope of salvation. Muslims with learning disabilities have an automatic hope of salvation. The nature of their resurrection bodies, though, is uncertain.

Thus there are clear differences between the perspectives. These, in turn, have implications for outreach to the disabled. For Muslims, their primary motive is the fulfilment of duties, and this involves practical steps to care and cater for those with disabilities. Al-Basit states, "Islam views services rendered to the disabled and assisting them as good deeds, which help one to get closer to the Exalted, the Almighty, and as charity, which deserves a reward."[175] But for Evangelicals, their primary motive is a heart for sharing the Gospel

---

[173] C.G. Moucarry, 'Islam (Sunni)', in *Dictionary of Contemporary Religion in the Western World: Exploring Living Faiths in Postmodern Contexts* (ed. Christopher Partridge and Douglas Groothuis; Leicester: IVP, 2002), 253.

[174] 2, 186.

[175] Dr Musa al-Basit, *The Rights of the Physically and Mentally Challenged in the Islamic Shari'a*. As cited in Rispler-Chaim, *Disability in Islamic Law*, 132.

with this people group in a way that they can access,[176] since Jesus claims, "I am the resurrection and the life."[177]

Appendix 1: Useful Websites for Further Reference

Evangelical Organisations

Caring for Life: http://www.caringforlife.co.uk

Causeway Prospects: http://www.prospects.org.uk/index.php/causeway_prospects/1/1

Charnwood Nursery: http://charnwoodnursery.org.uk/index.htm

Through the Roof: http://www.throughtheroof.org

Islamic Organisations

Association of Muslims with Disabilities:
http://www.multikulti.org.uk/agencies/arabic/london/17807/index.html

Baseera Islamic Madrasa for the blind, deaf and children with special needs: http://www.baseera.co.uk

http://www.youtube.com/watch?v=OA5oLMH2zzg

Appendix 2: Causeway Statement

Causeway: A Christian ministry for people with a learning difficulty

Causeway is based on two main principles. Firstly, that all people should have an opportunity to hear the Christian message including those with a learning difficulty, and secondly, all people are capable of responding to the Christian message because it is a matter of belief and trust, not intellect and ability.

In the UK one in fifty people have a learning difficulty and Causeway seeks to befriend such people, explain the Christian

---

[176] It turns "pity, fear, and avoidance into empathy, quest, and involvement." Gene Newman and Joni Eareckson Tada, *All God's Children: Ministry to the Disabled* (Grand Rapids, Mich.: Zondervan, 1987), 23.

[177] John 11: 25.

message in a relevant way, and provide a sympathetic environment where people can respond to the message.

Causeway is a church based ministry affiliated to a national organisation called Prospects. Central to the work of Causeway at Haywards Heath Evangelical Free Church is a monthly meeting dedicated to people with a learning difficulty. Here friendships are built through spending time together, sharing experiences in a group setting, and personal conversations. The Bible is taught in an easy to understand way with the help of visual aids and drama. Opportunity is given to the group to respond to God through reading, singing, playing percussion instruments, and praying.

The meetings have been running since 1990 and many of the people who attend have grown in their awareness of God and have found personal fulfilment through believing and trusting in Jesus Christ. The Bible tells us that God has a special concern for the disadvantaged in society and there is clear evidence that through Causeway God is blessing people with a learning difficulty.

The main monthly meetings are usually held on the last Sunday of each month. The meetings run from 3.00pm to 4.30pm with the first hour taken up with singing, sharing, praying, and Bible teaching. The last half-hour is given over to refreshments and a time for personal conversations. Between 20 and 30 people, including team members, attend the meetings. People come from both Haywards Heath and Burgess Hill and from a range of situations including residential homes and supported living within the community.

The meetings are open to all people with a learning difficulty, not just those who attend church, and further information is available on telephone number 01444 459809. If you think these meetings could be of a benefit to you or a relative or friend then please do not hesitate to call us.

Integral Mission in a Disintegrating World

David Williams

2011 Leonard Buck Lecture, Melbourne School of Theology

Introduction

My aim this evening is to explore the theme of integral or holistic mission. I am going to use the term "integral mission" – some of you may be more familiar with the expression "holistic mission" – different terminology but the same meaning. Integral or holistic mission is the conviction that genuine mission must fully integrate, on the one hand proclamation, evangelism and disciple-making and on the other hand, social action and social justice. There is no doubt that "integral mission" is accepted orthodoxy in the majority of missiological writing. I want to suggest that the debate about whether mission is integral or not is far from over and that a number of emerging theological and missiological themes bring new dimensions to this conversation.

Before we begin to explore those themes, it is good to remember that the issues that we are talking about when we discuss integral mission are real issues about real people. I have Kenyan Christian friends who are living in the slums of Nairobi right now. I have friends in Christian leadership in Nairobi, both expatriate and Kenyan, who are struggling today with what is the right and appropriate missiological response to urban poverty. Some of what we are talking about this evening is theoretical – but poverty is not a theory. Millions of Christians around the world today are disempowered and trapped by grinding poverty.

So with that proviso in mind, let me chart a course for us. I want to begin by looking at some indicators that suggest that the debate about integral mission is very much alive and well. We'll then move on to examine four areas of contemporary theological reflection to ask what light they shed on the issue of integral mission. Finally I want to offer my own suggestion of a way forward. Let's begin by reviewing the current debate about integral mission.

Evangelism and Social Action: the Lausanne Conversation[178]

One way to track the recent debate about integral mission within evangelicalism is to look at the conversation that took place at last year's Lausanne conference in Cape Town.

In the years following the first Lausanne conference in 1974, holistic or integral mission has become accepted orthodoxy for many evangelicals. Chris Wright, convenor of the Theology Working Group for Lausanne 2010, endorses the following quote in his book *The Mission of God*:

> There is no longer a need to qualify mission as "holistic", nor to distinguish between "mission" and "holistic mission." Mission is, by definition, "holistic" and therefore "holistic mission" is, de facto, mission.[179]

Despite this assertion, it was clear at Cape Town that the debate over holistic mission is still alive and kicking. This was most evident in John Piper's Bible study on Ephesians 3[180]. Piper expounded the cosmic purpose of God, who makes known his wisdom to the demonic powers of the universe through the mystery of the gospel. Jews and Gentiles together are objects of God's wrath. God's abundant, overflowing love puts the Lord Jesus Christ between us and God's wrath. This reality confronts us with two truths: first, when the gospel takes root in our souls, it compels us out to share Christ's love. Second, when the gospel takes root in our souls, it awakens us to the horror of eternal perishing and impels us to proclaim "flee the wrath to come." Piper sought to recapture the language of the primacy of evangelism from article six of the original Lausanne covenant with the following proposition: "For Christ's sake, Christians care about all suffering, especially eternal suffering." But for people like Rene Padilla, the language of primacy is antithetical to holistic mission. Padilla argues that

---

[178] Some of the material in this section has been published in David Williams, 'Holistic Mission?' *Essentials*, Autumn (2011) 3-5, Evangelical Fellowship of the Anglican Communion.

[179] Christopher Wright, *The Mission of God* (Leicester: Inter-Varsity Press, 2007), 323.

[180] John Piper, 'Bible Expostion - Ephesians 3', 24 September, 2010. http://conversation.lausanne.org/en/conversations/detail/10970 (February 16, 2011).

evangelism and social justice are like the two wings of an aeroplane – without both wings a plane is not a functioning plane[181]. The language of primacy does not fit that metaphor – you can't have a plane where one wing is bigger and more important than the other.

The themes evident in Piper's address were also apparent in Ajith Fernando's exposition of Ephesians 1 and Vaughan Roberts' exposition of Ephesians 4. Both stressed the priority of word ministry, with Roberts pointing to a famine of the word of God today, arguing that there is no greater mission need than those who will minister God's word in the church and the world.

These comments reflected a reaction by conservatives to the integral mission issue. However, it is not only conservatives who are unhappy. Blogging after the conference, Rene Padilla has written of his frustration with the Cape Town commitment, the document that was the main outcome of the conference. His particular concern, as it was in 1974, is that the language of primacy remains evident, when in his opinion it should be completely removed. So he argues that the distinction between 'strengthening, inspiring and equipping the Church for the evangelisation of the world in our generation', but only 'exhorting Christians about their responsibility to participate in matters of public and social interest' reflects an unhelpful and non-holistic balance.[182] He would prefer the language about social action to be as strong as the language about evangelism and for the two to be viewed as entirely inseparable.

So what has changed between Lausanne 1974 and Cape Town 2010? Clearly, one massive change has been that in 1974 the majority view prioritised evangelism, while in 2010 integral mission was undoubtedly the majority position. In that sense, there has been a sea change between the two conferences. But in another sense little has changed – the debate was still conducted around the language of primacy or priority; the theological terms in which the debate was carried out have not changed much in 35 years; and to some extent the debate still set majority world missiologists against theologically conservative westerners. My concern with the

---

[181] C. Rene Padilla, *Mission between the Times* (Grand Rapids: Eerdmans, 1985), 198.

[182] Rene Padilla, 'Fundacion Kairos', 03 November, 2010.
http://www.kairos.org.ar/blog/?p=469 (October 12, 2011).

conversation that took place at the Cape Town conference was that we don't seem to have moved very far forward in the way that we are holding the debate. So much has changed and so much has happened in missiological thinking between 1974 and 2010. So let me pose a question: what new themes in missiology might inform our understanding of integral mission, bringing new perspectives and fresh insight? Let me share with you four different areas that have informed my own thinking.

Trinitarian Missiology

The first area that I'd like to explore is the theme of Trinitarian missiology, particularly from within an evangelical perspective. In my opinion, Timothy Tennent's book *Invitation to World Missions*[183] will quickly become the standard student textbook on the subject of mission. Tennent outlines what he calls the standard approach to writing about mission, which is to develop an understanding of mission in the light of biblical theology, church history and anthropology before moving into more practical application[184]. This traditional approach is similar to that taken by David Bosch in his classic work *Transforming Mission*[185]. Tennent argues that this kind of approach to writing about mission doesn't take the twin themes of the Trinity and of the *missio dei*, the mission of God, with sufficient seriousness. Studying mission should not be some conglomeration of disciplines with a few applications tacked onto the end. Nor should it be a marginal subject in an already crowded theological curriculum. Mission is not an optional extra, but rather it expresses the very character of God. So mission should not simply be a discipline within theology but should be the context within which all theology should be taught. This is in essence the same point that Chris Wright is making when he argues that we should not talk about a biblical theology of mission, but rather talk about the missional theology of the Bible[186].

---

[183] Timothy C. Tennent, *Invitation to World Missions - a Trinitarian Missiology for the 21st Century* (Grand Rapids: Kregel, 2010).

[184] Timothy C. Tennent, *Invitation to World Missions*, 65.

[185] David Bosch, *Transforming Mission* (New York: Orbis, 1991).

[186] Christopher Wright, *The Mission of God*, 29.

Tennent therefore structures the whole of his book around the persons of the Trinity, taking great care to argue that the mission of God and the mission of God's people are not the same thing. By developing the theme of *missio dei*, Tennent argues for a distinction between the words *mission* and *missions*. He suggests that we should use the word mission to refer to "God's redemptive, historical initiative on behalf of his creation".[187] So mission is the work of God, the *missio dei*, while missions is the work of God's people, the church. Tennent defines missions as:

... all the specific and varied ways in which the church crosses cultural boundaries to reflect the life of the triune God in the world and, through that identity, participates in his mission, celebrating through word and deed the in-breaking of the New Creation.[188]

This distinction between mission and missions helps to clarify that everything the church does must be founded on "the prior nature, character and initiative of God".[189]

But what exactly is this prior nature and character of the triune God? And how does the *missio dei* exactly relate to the Trinity? We have tended to relate the Trinity to mission through the sending action of God. God the Father sends his Son into the world in the incarnation of the Lord Jesus. The Father and the risen Lord Jesus send the Spirit into the world. This sending activity within the Trinity then becomes the model of mission as the church is sent into the world.

In his challenging work, *The Witness of God*[190], John Flett seeks to develop a more nuanced understanding of the missionary nature of the Trinity. Flett argues that the *missio dei* is fundamentally about the person and nature of God and not simply about God's activity. God reconciles the world to himself because of who he is, his very identity. In other words the *missio dei* is about the triune God's *being* not just about his *doing*[191]. God is by his very nature missionary –

---

[187] Timothy C. Tennent, *Invitation to World Missions*, 59.

[188] Timothy C. Tennent, *Invitation to World Missions*, 59.

[189] Timothy C. Tennent, *Invitation to World Missions*, 488.

[190] John Flett, *The Witness of God* (Grand Rapids: Eerdmans, 2010).

[191] John Flett, *The Witness of God*, 201.

the loving work of reconciling the world to himself is all about the very character and nature of the triune God.

Let me try and give a simple illustration. My children might observe that from time to time I come home and give my wife a bunch of flowers. But if they consider that simply to be an action that should be mimicked in other situations, they will have failed to understand the nature of my marriage relationship. Giving flowers to my wife is an action. But it is an action that flows out of a relationship, indeed a God-given, one-flesh relationship. So giving flowers to my wife is quite different to giving flowers to a sick friend or a retiring colleague or a prize winning student. Giving flowers to my wife is an action that flows out of a fundamental relationship. In the same way, God's redemptive, historical initiative on behalf of creation is an action that flows out of the fundamental relationship of the triune God. Mission flows from the character and relationship of the Trinity.

This has profound implications for the church, the people of God. Flett argues that just as God is missionary by his very nature, so the church, if it is truly the church, is also missionary by its very nature. Flett writes:

> As God's deliberate turning to the world belong to his own being, so the church's deliberate turning to the world belongs to her relationship with him. It is not an act an otherwise constituted church may or may not choose to perform.[192]

And quoting Barth:

> "The community is as such a missionary community, or she is not the Christian community." She is missionary by her very nature because the God she serves is missionary.[193]

All too often in our churches, mission becomes an activity that is tagged onto any number of other activities, when it should be fundamental to who we are. All too often in our theological colleges, although I'm sure not here at MST, mission is an optional extra, a curriculum subject of peripheral importance, when it should be the defining paradigm within which all our theology is taught. Mission is fundamental to the very nature and character of God – it

---

[192] John Flett, *The Witness of God*, 204.

[193] John Flett, *The Witness of God*, 285.

is who he is. This is the language of Deuteronomy 7 – God chose the people of Israel because he loved. It was nothing to do with them. It was all about the person and character of God himself. God is missionary. And so for God's people, in relationship with the triune God. We are to be missionary by our very nature. Mission is fundamentally who we are.

So here is my first proposition:

Proposition One: Mission flows from the triune God who is missionary by his very nature. So God's people, in relationship with the triune God, are to be missionary by their very nature.

Let's move on to look at the theme of continuity and discontinuity.

Continuity and Discontinuity

I became a Christian in 1983. I look back with great gratitude on the discipleship that I received as a young Christian and for the firm grounding that I was given in God's Word. My memory, as I look back on those first years of my Christian life, is that I was taught that the great hope of the gospel is that when I died I would go to heaven to be with Jesus. I was pretty hazy about what that meant, but I think my principle understanding was that my soul would be with Jesus in heaven.

Fast forward nearly 30 years, and I think that contemporary evangelical theology has helped us to move towards a more truly biblical eschatology. Tom Wright, amongst others, has helped us to be much clearer that the great hope of the gospel is not disembodied souls in heaven, but resurrection bodies in the new creation. As Wright says:

> My proposition is that the traditional picture of people going to heaven on the one hand or going to hell on the other ... represents a serious distortion and diminution of the Christian hope. Bodily resurrection is not just one odd bit of that hope. It is the element which gives shape and meaning to the rest of the story we tell about God's ultimate purposes. If we squeeze it to the margins, as many have done by implication, if indeed if we leave it out altogether, as some have done quite explicitly, we don't just lose an extra component of the machine, like choosing to buy a car which happens not to have electrically operated mirrors. We lose the central engine which drives it and gives every other component its reason for working. Instead of talking vaguely about "heaven" and then trying to fit the language of resurrection into that, we should talk with

biblical precision about the resurrection, and reorganise our language about heaven around that.[194]

For me, this has made Christian hope somehow more hopeful, more wonderful, more imaginable. And I'd add that it is an expression of Christian hope that I think is more biblically faithful.

One consequence of this eschatological debate has been a revisiting of the themes of continuity and discontinuity between this creation and the new creation. This has been much debated within evangelical missiology. If we were to parody the argument we would create two opposing camps – radical discontinuity and radical continuity. The view of radical discontinuity would be that everything in our world is going to be burned up, so we should focus on saving souls because they are the only thing that will last. The view of radical continuity would say that everything in this earth lasts into the new creation, so everything has eternal value, significance and worth.

But as I said, those are parodies. The on-going debate about the exact nature of continuity or discontinuity is nuanced and ties in many different theological themes. A number of those developing a theology of continuity come from a strongly reformed and Calvinistic perspective. For example, Richard Mouw from Fuller Theological Seminary has engaged with the continuity conversation from the perspective of Calvin's theology of common grace[195]. David Field, until recently at Oak Hill Theological College, has also written helpfully on this subject[196]. In a lecture that seeks to address the statement that "all that really matters is evangelism because nothing else lasts", Field argues for the continuity of the works of the people of God from this creation to the new creation. He writes:

> When believers, in the power of the Spirit and in union with Christ, obey the commandments of God, when they exercise their faith through love, then they are being a new creation and doing new creation deeds. These things have their place the other side of judgement day for the very reason that they have, with the Spirit, so

---

[194] Nicholas T. Wright, *Surprised by Hope* (London: SPCK, 2007), 160.

[195] Richard Mouw, *He Shines in all that's Fair: Culture and Common Grace* (Grand Rapids: Eerdmans, 2001).

[196] David Field, '*Not the Least Lash Lost*', January, 2007. http://davidfield.com/other/AAPC2-3lecture.pdf (October 12, 2012).

to speak "come from the future" into the present. The fruit of the Spirit is imperishable – it does not have a sell-by date. These things belong to the new heavens and new earth and therefore will not pass away.[197]

This points us to one of the key lessons that flows out of the focus of the continuity argument, which is to stress the significance of God's people now as an eschatological foretaste of the new creation. Any continuity between this creation and the new creation is only a continuity in Christ and because of Christ. Passages in the New Testament that talk about the redemption of creation, Colossians 1 and Romans 8 for example, make it explicit that the redemption of creation is in Christ and through his death on the cross. Biblical continuity into the new creation is continuity *in Christ*. Those human beings who are not in Christ face their own continuity into eternal punishment and separation from God. Evangelism is not de-prioritised by an appropriate focus on continuity – if anything the continuity argument strengthens the logic of eternal punishment for those who do not know Christ. So if a theology of continuity is not to become universalist, it must stress that continuity is in Christ. God's people who are in Christ are a new creation, and we are called to live the life of the new creation now. So the lives of God's people in the present are an eschatological foretaste of God's new world order.

So to my second proposition:

Proposition Two: Continuity between this earth and the new creation is continuity only in Christ. So God's people, in Christ, are to be an eschatological foretaste of the new creation.

Culture and Change

The third area I want to explore is the role that the Church plays in engaging with and transforming secular culture. Perhaps the most significant works in this area recently are Andy Crouch's *Culture Making*[198] and James Davison Hunter's book *To Change the World*[199] While Hunter and Crouch do not necessarily agree on a definition

---

[197] Field, David. *Not the Least Lash Lost.* http://davidfield.com/other/AAPC2-3lecture.pdf (October 12, 2012).

[198] Andy Crouch, *Culture Making* (Downers Grove: Inter-Varsity Press, 2008).

[199] James Davison Hunter, *To Change the World,* (Oxford: Oxford University Press, 2010).

of culture[200], they do reach common ground in critiquing an over-optimistic expectation of the impact that individual Christians have on secular society. In particular, they demonstrate the fallacy behind the argument that if enough individuals become Christians in a particular society, then that society will inevitably be changed. While Crouch and Hunter focus fairly specifically on the North American context, this is a reality that is easily illustrated from other parts of the world. In Kenya, for example, over 30% of the population would profess to be born again and around 80% would call themselves Christians. But this weight of numbers has done almost nothing to stem the tide of rampant corruption that exists on a systemic scale. It is self-evident that culture and society are not automatically transformed just by individuals becoming Christians. In fact, culture is both formed and changed by institutions that are at the cultural centre of society. The view that individuals change culture without reference to these central institutions is, according to Hunter, "almost wholly mistaken".[201]

Crouch and Hunter move towards similar conclusions as to how to address these issues. Both argue that God's people should stop trying to change the world or transform the culture and should rather focus on being the community that God intends them to be. Crouch puts it like this:

> My hope is to move the conversation entirely away from "strategies" of cultural change. The reason to be culture makers is not "to change the world" or "to transform the culture." It is *to be who we were created to be:* stewards of a good world, bearing the image of a creative God who always intended us to cultivate and create in that world. Can God use our local, embodied efforts at culture making to "change the world"? Surely he can, if he wishes to do so.[202]

Hunter develops his argument around the concept of "faithful presence." He argues that the pluralist, post-Christian culture of the 21st Century is an environment that God's people have never encountered before. Contemporary Christian attempts to transform secular culture tend to employ one of a variety of political

---

[200] James Davison Hunter, *To Change the World*, 27-30.

[201] James Davison Hunter, *To Change the World*, 17.

[202] Andy Crouch, *Christianity Today*, 14 May, 2010. http://www.christianitytoday.com/ct/2010/mayweb-only/29-51.0.html (October 12, 2011).

methodologies that have implicitly sold out to the cultures that they are trying to critique. Christians should rather focus on their life as the community of God's people, living passionately and wholly for God in every sphere of their lives. Living for God means employing the methodologies of God – so the heart of Christian engagement needs to be the sacrificial, daily taking up our cross to follow Jesus. Both Crouch and Hunter agree that the first priority of God's people must be to live faithfully for him and to trust his sovereign rule to take care of the bigger picture. The world will not be changed by Christians trying to change the world but by Christians being the community of people God has called us to be. Hunter puts it like this:

> Thus, when the Word of life is enacted within the whole body of Christ in all of its members through an engagement that is individual, corporate and institutional, not only does the word become flesh, but an entire lexicon and grammar becomes flesh in a living narrative that unfolds in the body of Christ; a narrative that points to God's redemptive purposes. It is authentic because it is enacted and finally persuasive because it reflects and reveals the shalom of God.[203]

Crouch makes a similar point in more straight forward language:

> So do you want to make culture? Find a community, a small group who can lovingly fuel your dreams and puncture your illusions. Find friends and form a family who are willing to see grace at work in one another's lives, who can discern together which gifts and which crosses each has been called to bear. Find people who have a holy respect for power and a holy willingness to spend their power alongside the powerless. Find some partners in the wild and wonderful world beyond church door. And then, together, make something of the world.[204]

While Crouch and Hunter are not in total agreement, I think they are making the same fundamental point: Christian engagement in cultural transformation flows out of the life of the community of God's people.

So my third proposition is this:

---

[203] James Davison Hunter, *To Change the World*, 254.

[204] Andy Crouch, *Culture Making*, 263.

Proposition Three: Christians cannot change the world by using the world's methods. God's people change the world by being the communities He calls us to be.

Post-Christendom Missiology

The fourth area that I'd like to explore is the theme of post-Christendom mission. This is an issue of particular concern for churches in Europe, Canada, Australia and New Zealand where we are most clearly living in "Post-Christendom." These are the countries where the Church is living in a context that once had a deep historic Christian heritage, but where that heritage is now being forgotten. Stuart Murray defines post-Christendom as ...

> ... the culture that emerges as the Christian faith loses coherence within a society that has been definitively shaped by the Christian story and as the institutions that have been developed to express Christian convictions decline in influence.[205]

This is a new reality, never faced by God's people before. The early Church existed in a *pre*-Christian context. A *post*-Christian context carries some of the ignorance of the Christian message that existed in a pre-Christian situation, but also struggles with the negative assumptions inherited from Christendom. Some of the negative issues that are part of a Christendom heritage include the crusades, institutionalised paedophilia, abuse of power, the relationship between church and state, the list could go on and on.

Murray outlines some of the transitions that are taking place for Churches as we move into a post-Christendom world.

> God's people are moving from the centre to the margins, from the majority to the minority, from settlers to sojourners, from privilege to plurality, from control to witness, from maintenance to mission, from institution to movement.[206]

In the last 12 months we have seen this reality at work in some obvious ways right here in Melbourne: the lawsuit against the Christian conference centre at Phillip Island, the sustained attack on Access ministries and school chaplaincy, the current threat to the tax deductible status of mission agencies in the Federal tax review.

---

[205] Stuart Murray, *Post-Christendom* (Carlisle: Paternoster Press, 2004), 19.

[206] Stuart Murray, *Post-Christendom*, 20.

These kinds of examples will only increase in the years ahead. Many privileges that Churches have considered to be their right will be removed. Our right to speak into public life will increasingly be questioned.

One of the consequences of the Christendom mindset was a separation of local church and mission. Mission was something that was done by specialist agencies overseas. In a Christendom mindset, the home country was Christian, the mission field was overseas, with the consequence that the local congregation was disconnected from mission.[207] Jehu Hanciles, a Sierra Leonean Professor teaching at Fuller, puts it like this:

> Informed by notions of Christendom, the Western missionary movement conceived of faith in territorial terms and fostered an understanding of Christian mission in which the world is territorially or geographically divided into church and mission field. This approach engendered a unidirectional flow of resources and ideas in which the West was the sender and the non-West the receiver. Within the emergent non-Western movement, however, each nation sends as well as receives missionaries. Never before has the course of missionary movement been this multi-directional, disparate and global. In particular, African Christians conceive of the whole world (including Africa itself) as a mission field. Additionally, the African missionary movement is a church-based initiative that promotes church-centred engagement. This emphasis diverges sharply from the European missionary movement which emerged outside the existing church structures, operated almost exclusively through extra-ecclesial missionary orders or voluntary societies and produced an entrenched church/mission dichotomy in both missiology and mission praxis.[208]

The emerging mission movements that are coming out of Africa are very largely church based. Attempts to found mission agencies in Africa that resemble traditional western mission agencies have not generally been very successful. Hanciles is, I think, right to react against attempts that impose western categories on African and Majority World mission. So while he generally applauds the work of Philip Jenkins[209], he rejects the suggestion that Africa is "the next

---

[207] Stuart Murray, *Post-Christendom*, 130.

[208] Jehu Hanciles, *Beyond Christendom* (New York: Orbis, 2008), 390.

[209] Philip Jenkins, *The Next Christendom: the Coming of Global Christianity* (Oxford: Oxford University Press), 2002.

Christendom" – why would we want to impose the failed category of Constantinian Christendom on emerging African mission? Mission in Africa is rightly church-based, church-initiated, church-driven. And for us living in "Post-Christendom," recovering the missional character of the church as the church's very essence is perhaps one of the most critical challenges we face. In Christendom, the Church could exist in maintenance mode, but post-Christendom does not allow us that possibility. One of the roots of the emerging / emergent church conversation is about what a Post-Christendom missional church should look like.

So my fourth proposition is this:

Proposition four: In Post-Christendom, the Church has moved from the centre to the margins, from the majority to the minority. So God's people must be missionary by their very nature if they are to stay in existence.

Here then are my four propositions:

1) God's people, in relationship with the triune God, are to be missionary by their very nature.

2) God's people, in Christ, are to be an eschatological foretaste of the new creation.

3) God's people change the world by being the community of people He calls us to be.

4) In Post-Christendom, God's people must be missionary by their very nature if they are to stay in existence.

From Integral Mission to Integral Church

Let me try to draw these different strands together and apply them to our understanding of integral mission. Each of these strands has stressed in different ways the inseparable relationship between mission and church. And each has in its own way stressed that the church is missional or missionary by its very nature.

One of the problems in our debate about integral mission is that the engagement of the church is often marginalised. We know theoretically that when we talk about integral mission, we are talking about the integral mission *of the church*. But all too often those last three words, *of the church*, get assumed, or taken for granted, or ignored. This creates problems in two directions.

Heading in one direction, we see organisations who say that they are doing integral mission, but whose activities bear little or no connection with the church. I can think of a variety of organisations both in Western countries and in Majority World countries, who would say that they are doing integral mission, but whose activities have minimal connection with local churches and who have staff teams where only a quarter would profess to be followers of the Lord Jesus.

Heading in the other direction, we see local churches who think that integral mission has nothing much to do with them. They view integral mission as something that happens elsewhere, probably overseas, and is done by others, usually a mission agency. Integration, holism, is not on their agenda.

I want to suggest that in the integral mission debate, we have attached the word "integral" to the wrong noun. We have spent a long time discussing the integral mission of the church. We would do better, I think, to talk about the mission of the integral church. The thing that God intends to be integral or holistic is not simply the outreach activity of Christians or churches. Rather, the integration of word and deed is located within the life of the local community of God's people. It is the life of the local church that is supposed to be an integrated whole, the body of Christ.

So rather than "the integral/holistic mission of the church" I am suggesting that we should talk about "the mission of the integral/holistic church." This is not just semantic. Rather, it helps us to reflect the themes we have been developing, which stress that God's people are to be missionary by their very nature, an eschatological foretaste of the new creation.

My hope is that by talking about the mission of the integral church, we might be able to address the false dichotomy between word and deed. The focus on care for the poor, advocacy for the oppressed and needy, justice and compassion is an undeniable and central theme within Scripture. But this theme is located within the community of God's people. God's people, in both the Old and the New Testament, are to be a community who care for the poor and seek justice for the oppressed. They are to care for those within their community, for those on the margins of the community and for any whom God brings into their sphere of influence.

However, the way that God forms these gathered, integrated, holistic, communities is through the ministry of His word. Faith comes by hearing the word of God (Romans 10:17). It is only the sword of the Spirit of God that has the power to draw men and women into relationship with God and then into reconciled community with one another. If we see word and deed as two different actions we inevitably set them in dichotomy against one another. However, if the aim of the ministry of the word is to create and build the holistic community of God's people, we avoid this separation.

Stressing the mission of the integral church also helps to address our tendency towards individualism. The redemption story of the Bible is the story of scattering and gathering as God draws together a chosen people. Christopher Ash develops a biblical theology around the themes of scattering and gathering, which helps us once again to see the central importance of the community of God's people in the biblical narrative.[210] The local church is the living, visible evidence of God's plan to finally gather all things to himself. As Ash says:

> The ordinary local church with all its imperfections, weaknesses, oddities and problems has within it the seeds, the spiritual and relational genetic blueprint, of a broken world remade. Here at last is not just God restraining human strife, but God actively gathering. There is in the church not just a treatment delaying the onset of scattering, but a cure actively replacing scattering with gathering.[211]

This is God's great plan – to gather together these strange, imperfect little communities that are the body of Christ. It is these communities, formed by God's Word that are to be integral and holistic.

> You are a chosen race, a royal priesthood, a holy nation, a people for his own possession, that you may proclaim the excellencies of him who called you out of darkness into his marvellous light. Once you were not a people, but now you are God's people; one you had not received mercy, but now you have received mercy (1 Peter 2:9-10).

---

[210] Christopher Ash, *Remaking a Broken World* (Milton Keynes: Authentic Media), 2010.

[211] Christopher Ash, *Remaking a Broken World*, 138.

Notes for Contributors

Submission requirements:

Manuscript

(1) Papers should not exceed 5000 words, although the Editor retains the discretion to publish papers beyond this length.

(2) It is preferable that submissions be prepared in Microsoft Word format.

(3) All papers are to be written in English, and an English transliteration given to any quotations or short phrases in original language.

(4) Authors are advised to use gender inclusive and non-discriminatory language.

(5) Any visuals should be integrated into the document, or sent separately as separate jpg or gif files with an explanation as to their position in the paper.

(6) Footnotes and bibliography should follow the style used in previous issues of this Occasional Paper series.

Submission

(1) Papers to be considered for inclusion are to be submitted directly to the Editor.

(2) Submissions are to be forwarded via electronic mail to csiof@mst.edu.au. If submitting within Australia, a hard copy must also be posted to CSIOF, PO Box 6257 Vermont Sth, Vic 3133.

(3) A declaration that the submitted articles are your own work and that you've acknowledged the work/s of others used in the articles in the references, etc. must be included with any submission.

(4) A covering letter that includes the authors' names, titles, affiliations, with complete mailing addresses, including email, telephone and facsimile numbers should be attached to the paper.

Review of Submissions

(1) All submissions will be sent to referees for anonymous recommendation.

(2) The Editor holds the right to make editorial corrections to accepted submissions.

Copyright

The CSIOF Occasional Papers series is published by the Melbourne School of Theology Press. The copyright for any published papers will remain with the author. MST publishes these papers on the following conditions:

- They do not appear elsewhere (including web pages) for 180 days from the date of publication in the CSIOF Occasional Papers series.
- Whenever they are printed elsewhere (including web pages), the following notice will be included: "This article first appeared in the __ issue of the *CSIOF Occasional Papers* series".
- We retain the right to use the paper in any CSIOF publications, reprints, or in electronic form (ie. Online, CD-Rom, etc.).
- We retain the right to use a portion or description of the paper with your name in our promotional material.
- Authors are themselves responsible for obtaining permission to reproduce copyright material from other sources.
- The author will be presented with two copies of the publication.

Disclaimer

The opinions and conclusions published in the CSIOF Occasional Papers series are those of the authors and do not necessarily represent the views of the Editor or the CSIOF. The Occasional Papers serve purely as an information medium, to inform interested parties of religious trends, discussion and debates. The Occasional Papers do not intend in any way to actively promote hatred of any religion or its followers.

www.ingramcontent.com/pod-product-compliance
Lightning Source LLC
Chambersburg PA
CBHW051434290426
44109CB00016B/1548